Technical Change
and Employment

Technical Change and Employment

Roy Rothwell and Walter Zegveld

Foreword by Christopher Freeman

Frances Pinter, London

Copyright©Science Policy Research Unit, University of Sussex, U.K.
and The Organisation for Applied Scientific Research,
Netherlands 1979

First published in Great Britain in 1979 by
Frances Pinter (Publishers) Limited
5 Dryden Street, London WC2E 9NW

ISBN 0 903804 55 7

Printed in Great Britain by A. Wheaton & Co. Ltd., Exeter

CONTENTS

Foreword by Christopher Freeman   vii

1. THE PROBLEM   1

2. THEORETICAL ASPECTS OF TECHNICAL
   CHANGE AND EMPLOYMENT   15

3. STRUCTURAL CHANGES IN POST-WAR
   PATTERNS OF EMPLOYMENT   37

4. PATTERNS OF UNEMPLOYMENT   53

5. CASE STUDIES OF THE IMPACT OF TECHNICAL
   CHANGE ON EMPLOYMENT   61
   - 5(i)   Agriculture   62
   - 5(ii)   Mechanization of the U.K. Coal Mining
     Industry   67
   - 5(iii)   Canadian Railways   76
   - 5(iv)   The Textile Machinery Industry   79
   - 5(v)   The Textile Industry   83
   - 5(vi)   The Cement Industry   97
   - 5(vii)   The Steel Industry   103
   - 5(viii) The Metalworking Industry   108
   - 5(ix)   Numerically Controlled Machine Tools   114
   - 5(x)   Computer-Aided Design   118

| | 5(xi) | Automation | 122 |
| | 5(xii) | Analysis | 129 |

6. THE IMPACT OF MICROELECTRONICS ON
EMPLOYMENT 133
	6(i)	Watch-making Industry	136
	6(ii)	Word Processing and Automation in the Office	138
	6(iii)	Microelectronics in the Printing Industry	146
	6(iv)	The Telecommunications Industry	152
	6(v)	The Textile and Textile-machinery Industries	153
	6(vi)	Microelectronics and Automation	156
	6(vii)	Microelectronics and the Self-Service Economy	161
	6(viii)	Summary	162

Appendix: The Impact of Microelectronics on
Assembly and Negative Multiplier
Effects 164

7. SUMMARY OF MAIN POINTS 167

Index 175

ACKNOWLEDGEMENTS

The authors wish to acknowledge the contributions to this study made by the participants of the Six Countries Programme Workshop in Paris, and especially those who presented papers at the Workshop.

The authors wish particularly to acknowledge the contribution of Professor Christopher Freeman whose pioneering work in this field contributed greatly to Chapters 1 and 2 of this study.

Finally, thanks are due to Dr Ard Bogers for his many useful suggestions during several discussions.

FOREWORD

This book emerged from the Six Countries Programme on Aspects of Government Policies towards Technological Innovation in Industry. As this programme is certainly not widely known and as the title hardly conveys the nature of its work, I shall attempt in this brief introductory note to outline its aims and origins.

During the 1960s and 1970s the problems of stimulating, managing and regulating technical innovation assumed increasing importance for industrial and economic policy. At the same time interest in these problems in the academic world was also growing. On the one hand policy-makers in various government departments and agencies wished to have access to the results of recent research and to discuss their implications for policy. On the other hand the researchers wished to discuss policy issues with those actively involved in government and to gain some access to their considerable experience in assessing the effectiveness and limitations of a range of old and new policy instruments.

This convergence of interests led to a successful attempt to bring the two streams together within the framework of a small international project, which in concept and in mode of operation had some of the characteristics of a small informal club. The original participants in 1974 came from four countries — the Netherlands, Germany, France and U.K. — and they were later joined by colleagues from Ireland and Canada in 1975.

The countries and their organisations concerned with the programme are:

Canada	Ministry of Industry, Trade and Commerce
France	Ministère de l'Industrie et de la Recherche *and* Secrétariat d'Etat à la Recherche
West Germany	Institut für Systemtechnik und Innovationsforschung
The Netherlands	Ministry of Economic Affairs *and* the Organisation for Applied Scientific Research (TNO)
Ireland	Institute for Industrial Research and Standards
United Kingdom	Department of Industry

The first stage of this project involved the commissioning of a major survey of the previous findings of relevant research in the field of interest. The results of this review by Keith Pavitt and William Walker were published in the journal *Research Policy* (volume 5, No. 1, pages 11–97) in January 1976. Following upon this preliminary stage a number of themes were selected for joint study and discussion and on the initiative and under the stimulating chairmanship of Walter Zegveld (TNO) the project took the form of a series of international seminars to discuss these topics.

Among the themes selected for these meetings were the role of small firms in innovation, the experience of direct subsidies for industrial research and development, and the experience of government regulation on technical innovation. Some papers were contributed from each of the participant countries and others from invited specialists with experience in the particular field of interest. The formula proved a successful one and outside interest grew.

Particularly great interest was shown in the two-day seminar held in Paris in November 1978 on the theme of technical change and employment. Over a hundred people attended this meeting, so that it assumed the dimensions of a small conference rather than a club seminar. Because of this great and continuing interest, both in the six countries and in many others, it was decided to publish the summary report of the meeting in book form.

In preparing this report it was decided not simply to publish excerpts from the various papers, as these papers were in any case available in full to researchers, albeit in mimeographed form. The project preferred rather to commission an edited review of the whole proceedings of the seminar, taking into account also other relevant contemporary research.

Dr Roy Rothwell, a Senior Fellow in the Science Policy Research Unit at the University of Sussex, was requested to undertake this difficult task in collaboration with Walter Zegveld, Head of the TNO staff group Strategic Surveys. In setting the timetable for preparation and publication of the book, they had in mind the rapid changes going on in the world as well as the requirements of project participants. They took the view that a book published fairly quickly, without all the 'i's being dotted and all the 't's crossed, would be of much more value to everyone than a more polished publication appearing a year or two later. They rose to the occasion and have produced very quickly an excellent report, which I am confident represents a timely contribution to the world-wide debate on this theme. Other colleagues in SPRU and TNO made helpful inputs, especially Ard Bogers of TNO.

The book sets out to analyse and explain the past, current and likely future impacts of technical change on employment. It does not attempt to discuss alternative social and political steps which might be taken as part of the adjustment process.

The Science Policy Research Unit has been associated with the Six Countries Programme from its inception and I am particularly glad that Roy Rothwell was able to make this contribution in association with his TNO colleagues. All of us are indebted to Walter Zegveld for his inspiring personal involvement in this and all other aspects of the programme.

CHRISTOPHER FREEMAN
Director, Science Policy Research Unit,
University of Sussex

CHAPTER 1

THE PROBLEM

This book deals with past and future trends of employment and unemployment in mature industrialized societies. Governments of these countries have become increasingly concerned about these problems, especially as it became apparent that the recovery of the world economy from the 1974–75 recession did not lead to a rapid fall in unemployment, which had been the pattern of all previous post-war recoveries.

Throughout Europe levels of unemployment have remained high by post-war standards following this recession period, and rose even higher in 1976–78 in a number of European countries.

In the United States, although the level of unemployment in the 1970s has been higher than in the 1960s, there was nevertheless some reduction during the 1976–78 period. As the labour force has been increasing fairly rapidly during this period this does reflect much success in generating new jobs through active employment policies and expansionary economic policies.

Varying national experiences are not of course the only basis for differing perceptions of unemployment problems, nor do theoretical differences necessarily follow national lines. Nevertheless, it probably is true to say that today there is greater interest in Europe in problems of structural change and technical change, whilst in the United States, in spite of the Carter Administration's current Domestic Policy Review on Innovation, the emphasis is more on aggregate demand. British, Dutch,

1

French and German papers at the recent OECD Conference on unemployment in 1977 all emphasized long-term structural problems, as well as problems of demand management.

In the 1950s and early 1960s, the positions were partly reversed. At that time unemployment was generally very low throughout Europe, whilst in the United States unemployment was relatively high. There was also considerable concern in the American Trade Unions about the effects of automation and computerization on levels of employment. This led at that time to the appointment of the U.S. National Commission on Technology, Automation and Economic Progress, whose report was published in 1966. The Commission heard evidence from a great many sources and sparked off a considerable debate on technical change and employment. On the whole the predominant view in this debate was that the unemployment problem in the U.S.A. was overwhelmingly one of demand, rather than one of structural or technical change.

In any case U.S. policy has in fact become much more expansionary since and U.S. growth rates were significantly higher in the 1960s than in the 1950s. Unemployment fell and there was a widespread feeling that the 'automation' scare had been a false alarm. It seemed quite possible to generate new jobs in sufficient numbers to offset any labour displacement involved in the adoption of new technology and in the shake-out of more traditional industries.

A critical question to ask now is: are there new features in the world economic situation and in world technology which mean that the employment problems of the 1980s will differ significantly from those encountered in the 1960s? A closely related question is: should the unemployment of the 1970s be written off as due to a period of demand deficiency − a purely temporary aberration from a steady long-term growth pattern? Or should the 1970s be regarded as marking a transition to rather different long-term patterns of development and employment?

In trying to answer these questions this book will present an argument for a 'structuralist' interpretation of some con-

2

temporary problems, and will argue that although of course aggregate demand is extremely important, explanations and prescriptions formulated purely in terms of aggregate demand are an insufficient guide. We will argue that the rate and direction of technical change cannot be dismissed as irrelevant to the issue of levels of employment, nor even as a peripheral issue, but must be accepted as one of the central issues involved.

If we examine long-term changes in the sectoral distribution of employment in mature industrial countries over the past quarter-century, then certain common trends are clearly discernible.

Some of these changes are well known: they are the steady decline of employment in the primary sectors — agriculture and mining — and the steady rise of employment in the tertiary or service sectors of the economy, both private and public. These trends are clearly evident in all major industrial countries throughout the period 1948–73. It is important to note that the decline in agricultural employment has generally been accompanied by a rise in agricultural output, and a rapid rise in the capital intensity of agriculture. It is an important fact that a pattern of 'jobless growth' of output has been well established in a major economic sector for a long time.

When we consider the trend of employment in manufacturing, the pattern is not quite so clear cut or so consistent as in the primary and tertiary sectors. There are variations between countries and there are peculiarities in the direction and rate of change of employment growth over time. Nevertheless one generalization does clearly emerge: the rate of increase in manufacturing employment had already slowed down very markedly in almost all mature industrial countries well before 1973.

During the period 1973 to 1977, almost all industrialized countries have experienced an absolute decline in employment in manufacturing. This applies to the United States and Japan as well as to Europe. The fact that this decline had already begun in some countries before 1973, and that in all the major countries the growth of manufacturing employment was already slowing down in the 1960s, suggests that this change cannot simply be attributed to the OPEC crises and the resultant shocks to the world economy. It is most probably part of a long-term structural change in the pattern of output and employment.

As between the various sectors within manufacturing, there is a fairly consistent pattern for all the mature industrialized societies. Employment in textiles has declined almost everywhere, and there has also been some more recent tendency for employment in the food industries to decline. In the United States, the United Kingdom and the Netherlands some decline was also already evident in several other major industrial sectors before 1973. In Europe and Japan the growth of employment was particularly strong in chemicals, machinery and vehicles in the 1950s and in the 1960s, but in the 1973–77 period all major sectors shared in the decline.

These changes are clearly related on the one hand to demand factors and on the other hand to new competitive sources of supply. At the same time total demand for food and textiles in affluent societies, although it continues to expand, is not growing so rapidly as demand for durables – or for services. There is of course nothing sensational about this, and it had been remarked upon long before 1973. The expression 'post-industrial' society had been coined to describe the type of structural change which was in progress.

If we are trying to answer the question: are there major new features of the world economy which will affect future patterns of employment, then already part of the answer lies in this change with respect to employment in manufacturing.

A second major question is: can expansion of employment opportunities in the tertiary sector, which has been such a dominant and consistent feature of the labour market over the past 30 years, continue at a high rate in the 1980s?

There are three major factors affecting the trend of manufacturing employment in mature industrialized societies in addition to the trend of aggregate demand. These are: changes in the world-wide location of industry, changes in the relative cost of factors of production and technological changes affecting both products and production techniques. All of them are closely interrelated and together they make it rather improbable that manufacturing employment will ever again expand in Europe and North America as it did in the 1950s and 1960s.

Whilst manufacturing employment has been declining in the industrialized European countries and the U.S.A. since 1973, it has been growing very rapidly in the newly industrializing countries, notably Korea, Brazil, Mexico, Taiwan and India. It has also grown significantly in some of the 'developing countries' of Europe such as Greece, Yugoslavia and Bulgaria.

At the same time several of these newly industrializing countries have been rather successful in expanding their exports of manufactures and broadening the base of their export trade. It is no longer just a question of competition in textiles and foodstuffs, but increasingly now also in chemicals, metals, vehicles and capital goods.

It would be short-sighted and nationalistic to begrudge the newly industrializing countries their recent success. Moreover, the effects on employment in the older industrialized countries have so far been rather small and confined largely to one or two industries, especially textiles. But it would also be foolish to overlook that these effects may now become more widespread.

We are of course discussing here long-term trends, and the speed of change should not be exaggerated. In spite of intense competition over the past 20 years textile industries still exist in the older industrial countries, and some branches of these industries are flourishing, even though they employ much fewer people. They have survived by a dual process of accelerated technical change and increased capital intensity, which is exactly the response which economic theory would predict.

Revolutionary technical advances in spinning and weaving machinery, the introduction of new synthetic fibres and the associated machinery, and numerous technical changes in the dyeing and finishing trades have all contributed to the rationalization and survival of smaller but competitive industries.

There seems no reason to suppose that this will not also be the pattern of response in each branch of manufacturing as world competition intensifies. It is indeed already happening in such industries as steel, rubber, shipbuilding and chemicals.

We are therefore in a position to say categorically that there is one major new factor at work in the world economy in the 1970s, which will become steadily more important during the 1980s, affecting more and more industries. There seems hardly any reason to doubt that the pressure exerted by this factor will be to reduce employment in manufacturing in the older industrial countries for two reasons — first through the direct erosion of world market shares, and secondly through intensified pressure for labour-saving technical change of the rationalization type. Stronger aggregate world-wide demand in the 1980s might mitigate the first but could intensify the second.

Clearly the pressure for rationalization can only have this outcome if there does exist a spectrum of new and more efficient capital-intensive techniques which can be substituted for the older more labour-intensive techniques. If such techniques are not available now and in the future, then the decline of employment is likely to be more rapid, as the competitive position of the mature high wage economies would be undermined more rapidly.

In fact, it is a reasonable supposition that the trend of new technology will permit, next to a great variety of new products in general, a range of rather effective labour-saving, material-saving and energy-saving technical changes to be introduced in the older industrial countries in the 1980s. The microelectronic revolution is already having this effect in several branches of mechanical engineering, electrical engineering, printing and office equipment.

However, although the competition of some newly industrializing countries will be increasingly important in the 1980s, it has not been the major factor affecting employment. Much more important has been the competition between the industrialized countries themselves and their internal structural changes.

Pressures of international competition have been reinforced by domestic pressures in the same direction. The cost of labour

6

relative to capital rose very sharply in most European countries between 1955 and 1973 and the rate of profit fell.

At the same time the trend of social legislation made it increasingly difficult to continue to regard labour as a variable cost. The combined effect of these tendencies was to make firms more cautious in hiring additional labour, and to seek labour-saving technical change instead. This is reflected in the clear-cut change in the 1970s in the pattern of manufacturing investment, with a marked shift away from 'capacity extension' to 'rationalization' of existing production facilities.

According to this interpretation, therefore, the decline in manufacturing employment in the 1970s was not simply the consequence of lower growth rates and pressure of demand, but also reflected a strong pattern of structural and technical change. This pattern can be expected to exert even greater impact in the 1980s.

In completing our assessment of future structural changes in manufacturing employment we can discriminate three different and overlapping areas: (1) traditional industries such as textiles, steel, shipbuilding, car manufacturing, etc. Here rationalization as a result of international price competition plays a dominant role; (2) capital goods industries, including engineering goods — for example the introduction of numerical control features on machine tools. Here, international technical change competitiveness plays a dominant role; (3) industries producing a large range of new products. Firms in question here are of the highly innovative type or are new technological enterprises, for example in electronics and semiconductors. Here too, obviously technical change competitiveness is even more crucial.

All three areas have their own features of technical change induced employment or unemployment.

Technical change, or innovation, has an employment-generating effect as well as an employment-destroying effect. These two effects may take place in different geographical areas. This is one of the principal reasons why governments in mature technological societies are currently placing so much emphasis on developing so-called innovation policies.

7

It has been argued that the pattern of 'jobless growth' which has been characteristic of agriculture for a long time, may now become the normal pattern of development for mature European manufacturing industry too. Clearly this would mean a major structural change in the mature industrial economies and this alone would certainly justify re-examination of perspectives for employment and unemployment in the 1980s. But even if this diagnosis is accepted it would not in itself mean that the goal of full employment would remain an unattainable one in the 1980s.

It would, however, put the whole burden of attaining such a goal on the generation of new employment opportunities in the tertiary sector of the economy. How realistic is the expectation that a high rate of job creation can continue in this sector during the 1980s sufficient to absorb the increase in the labour force from demographic changes and from rising female participation rates, and also to absorb any labour displaced from the primary and secondary sectors of the economy?

For those with a strong faith in the self-adjusting mechanisms of the market, there is not necessarily any problem here and the example of the United States may be cited as evidence of the feasibility of generating millions of new jobs in a fairly short period in the tertiary sector between 1975 and 1978.

However, some cautionary observations should be made both about the general problems of new service employment and about the specific case of the United States. A high proportion of these new jobs were generated in the public sector, partly as a direct result of various job creation schemes, and partly from the continuing expansion of education and welfare activities, especially at state level (as opposed to federal). This has also been a common experience in Europe in the recent past with health services, education and various forms of environmental services undergoing rapid expansion. It is therefore clearly necessary to distinguish public sector service employment from private sector service employment, and to examine the problems of the future expansion of each of them separately.

Taking first public sector service employment. There are acute problems of measurement, but it is commonly agreed that labour productivity increases in this sector (and to a lesser extent also in the private service sector) have been a good deal lower than in agriculture or in manufacturing.

Yet they are very labour-intensive activities and wage and salary pressures for parity with other workers in percentage increases in incomes have been strong. This has two consequences. On the one hand it is clearly a major source of wage cost inflationary pressure. On the other hand it generates problems of the scale and control of public expenditure where these services are financed primarily through central and local government budgets and taxes. The 1978 Californian referendum is only one extreme example of what has become a widespread political tendency to resist further increases in taxation, and further increases in public expenditure on service employment. It is difficult to be sanguine about the probability of a reversal of this trend when the political pressures to reduce taxation have become so powerful, both in Europe and in the U.S.A., and where counter-inflationary policies to reduce budget deficits and curb public expenditures have also become strong. It would therefore seem to be rather unwise to pin great hopes on the expansion of public sector service employment in the 1980s.

It is on private sector service employment that the main hopes must be based for future expansion, and there is of course a measure of truth in the view that if aggregate demand is raised sufficiently, then the private expenditures generated must ultimately exert a demand for goods and services *somewhere* in the economic system and labour must be used to supply these goods and services. Even though it may not be obvious just where the new growth points might be, there will surely be such new areas of growing demand for labour.

Structuralists would not deny the ultimate long-term validity of this view. But they would in varying degrees point out that this adjustment process can be prolonged, and that there could in particular be a problem of 'capital shortage' unemployment,

9

arising from an accelerated growth in capital intensity of production caused, among others, by rationalization technical change. This possibility was, for example, explicitly recognized in the 'McCracken Report' (*Towards Full Employment and Price Stability*, OECD, 1977).

'Capital shortage' unemployment could be expected to occur after a long period during which wage cost pressures had given rise to an intensive search for labour-saving technical change induced through new investment. In these circumstances the rise in capital requirements might be such that there would be a mis-match between the available capital stock and the available labour supply. It might be difficult to stimulate private new investment on the necessary scale because of lowered profit expectations and the desire of entrepreneurs to channel new investment into cost-saving rationalization rather than into new capacity and new product extension.

Surveys of investment intentions and of the distribution of investment expenditures between machinery on the one hand, and buildings on the other, support the view that for some time now in the older industrial countries, the pattern of new investment in manufacturing has shifted markedly in the latter direction. Would it, however, be possible that large numbers of new jobs could be created in the private service sector at a relatively much lower capital cost per work-place, thus alleviating and overcoming the 'capital shortage' problem?

Up to a point this is occurring. Such service industries as tourism and catering have continued to expand employment in the 1970s with relatively low capital costs. However, the direction and rate of technical change deserve very serious consideration in the private service sector of the economy too. In the opinion of some observers the labour-saving impact of the microelectronic revolution may well be greater in some service sectors than in manufacturing itself. In particular the future of office employment deserves thorough study. It is already technically possible to dispense with paper-based office procedures and to substitute purely electronic information systems. Any such widespread tendency would clearly have major implications for office personnel. The comparative advantages of the new microcomputers and the new telecommunications technology would appear to be greatest in any activity which involves the routine (or even the non-routine) collection, storage, transmission and simple manipulation of vast quantities of daily transactions, such as those performed in banks, insurance companies and other financial services. Word processors and other electronic equipment already in use have demonstrated that they could lead to a labour-saving pattern of technical change in areas which we have grown accustomed to regard traditionally as sectors of very low capital intensity. The revolutionary labour-saving potential of technical change in printing and publishing is already well established.

At the same time, some private sector service activities are becoming increasingly vulnerable to international competitive pressures. Publishing, banking and insurance activities are becoming more 'footloose' as a result of developments in communications technology. So that although new employment may be generated in these and many other private sector service activities, the international location of this employment may change. The speed of such changes should not be exaggerated since the diffusion of these technologies is not all that fast, partly because of management and worker resistance. Temporarily employment may remain high as a safeguard, at least in the early stages, but the ultimate employment effects can be regarded as considerable.

In discussing technical change related employment effects in both manufacturing and services main emphasis is usually put on quantitative problems of employment. There is growing evidence to suggest that technical change is increasingly generating a mismatch between available and required skills and is changing the nature of work. There is ample reason to assume that technical change will continue to alter the contents of work in manufacturing as well as in services in such a way that quality of work will come under increased pressure. Steps such as work-integration, participation and adjusted financial compensation ought to be seriously considered. Better functioning

11

of the labour market and the availability of retraining programmes also are prerequisites in a period of rapid technical change.

High rates of structural change in combination with jobless growth in agriculture, mining and manufacturing is placing pressure on governments of mature technological societies for new and sometimes contradictory policy measures. Rationalization technical change and international price competitiveness, for example, result in the situation that the increased productivities can sometimes not be translated into higher wages or increased profits and subsequent taxation for the financing of public services.

This book has sought to indicate some of the problems of structural adjustment to new patterns of employment in the older industrial countries in the 1980s. It must be emphasized that it is not technical change itself which is the problem. On the contrary, it is much more probable that low rates of technical change, especially of the international technical change competitiveness type, accompany high rates of unemployment. The failure of an industrial country to sustain technical progress would be far more likely to cause, under the present liberal trade conditions, serious structural unemployment problems, than a high rate of technical change.

The direction of technical change is important as well as the rate and there is clearly a need for product and service innovations which will sustain the competitive position of the older industrial countries, whilst not pushing the capital intensity of production to a point where capital shortage unemployment becomes a deep-rooted problem. 'Human capital' and new technology associated with high skills offer the greatest opportunities for the growing labour force.

A number of the policies formulated by governments that can affect both the rate and direction of technical change, both of which will have an impact on the relationship between technical change and employment discussed above, have been described in some detail in previous reports prepared for the Six Countries Programme:

12

- *The Current International Economic Climate and Policies for Technical Innovation*, by C. Freeman, K. Pavitt, A. Bogers and W. Zegveld, November 1977.
- *Small and Medium Sized Manufacturing Firms: their Role and Problems in Innovation*, by R. Rothwell and W. Zegveld, June 1978.
- *Government Procurement Policies and Industrial Innovation*, by W. Overmeer and F. Prakke, December 1978.

CHAPTER 2

THEORETICAL ASPECTS OF TECHNICAL CHANGE
AND EMPLOYMENT*

According to Clark (1978) unemployment can be defined as a situation in which there are fewer jobs available than people wishing to work, at prevailing wage rates. This imbalance can be redressed by increasing the number of job opportunities or by reducing the demand for jobs. In this section the demand side will not be considered, and the issue will be why the number of jobs available does not necessarily change towards matching the given demand, and the role technical change plays in increasing or decreasing the mismatch between the two.

There are basically two different types of unemployment; 'cyclical' unemployment, which is related to changes in the aggregate level of demand, and 'structural' unemployment which is associated with changes in the nature of demand, international competitiveness and technology. These are discussed separately below.

(i) Aggregate demand theory

Cyclic unemployment is essentially short-term in nature. It is associated with periodic slumps in the economy which are reflected in under-utilization of the capital stock. Economic recovery takes place in due course, and unemployed workers are then re-absorbed.

*For a survey of the main economic interpretations of the relation between technical change and employment, see J. A. Clark (1978).

The aggregate demand theory of unemployment was propounded by Keynes. He argued that the level of employment in the short term was determined by the level of output, while output depended in turn on the level of effective demand. Thus, rather than prices and wages acting as dependent variables to ensure the full use of labour resources — as argued by neo-classical economists — the level of demand becomes the crucial factor. According to this theory governments can, through the expedient of stimulating demand, decrease levels of unemployment.

(ii) Structural change theory

Structural unemployment is related to fundamental changes in the economy and society. Among the various factors which have been emphasized are: shifting patterns of consumer demand; decline in the rate at which new products appear on the market; a growing mismatch between skills and employment needs; a shift of production, and hence employment, to low wage cost developing countries; changes in production technology and techniques. Thus, structural unemployment is essentially long-term in nature.

Broadly speaking, there are three basic interpretations which might account for the structural nature of current unemployment patterns:
— the classical and Marxist interpretation;
— the international competition explanation;
— the technical change interpretation.
The first interpretation is based on the classical view of the falling rate of profit and implies the inextricable evolution of economic society to a stationary no-growth level. According to recent neo-Marxist formulations (Van Rossem, 1978), a structural crisis will occur when the average rate of profit falls below the average return on government or treasury bonds. When this happens private investment will fall and money will be directed to no-risk government bonds. The enormous state debt and the increasing need for government money to provide investment

incentives do not allow the gap between the profit rate and the return on government bonds to close. As a result, capitalist economy collapses, unemployment soars and profit can be restored only through 'war destruction'.

According to Soete (1978), Keynes's views on the achievement of full employment through demand creation would also lead the marginal efficiency of capital to be reduced to approximately zero within a single generation. This would bring society to conditions of a quasi-stationary community where change and progress would result only from changes in technique, taste, population and institutions. Contrary to the neo-Marxist view, Keynes sees this as the most sensible means to get rid of many of the objectionable features of capitalism.

In the second interpretation (a neo-classical one), structural unemployment is primarily due to shifts in the 'scarce' factor of production — labour in the developed world — from stagnant (labour-intensive) sectors to sectors having potential for growth (capital-intensive). The final result of this process of the international division of labour is one of national specialization in relative factor abundant industries or products. All countries end up being better off.

According to this interpretation, unemployment in the developed world is only temporary and is due more often to past unwillingness to adjust under trade liberalization than to sudden increased competition from low wage cost countries.

The third interpretation sees technical change as the main element of structural unemployment, and has been developed in two distinct directions. The first, based on the Schumpeterian analysis of innovation and business cycles, explains today's unemployment in terms of job-displacing technical change and increased pressure in most Western countries over the past 20 years for capital using technical change. Because of the necessary time lag, this pressure did not begin to be felt until the mid-1960s (Freeman, 1978). The second direction emphasizes the long-term impact of continuous, 'clay-clay' technical change. That is, incremental, labour-saving change, which is continuously being embodied in successive vintages of equipment.

17

This model would result in a gradual decline in employment accompanied by an increase in efficiency (labour productivity), (Vandoorne and Meeusen, 1978).

(iii) Assessing the theories of employment

In a recent paper, and operating with a great deal of detailed statistical data, Soete (1978) has attempted a preliminary assessment of the validity of the above theories for explaining changes in level of employment. This section is based on Soete's paper.

(a) *Aggregate demand theory*

Table 2.1 shows production and employment in manufacturing industry in the OECD member countries between 1973 and 1978. It shows that, with the exception of the U.S.A., the industrial recovery from the 1975 depression has not been accompanied in any of the 'rich' OECD countries by a similar recovery in employment. In fact — again with the exception of the U.S.A. — in all the rich OECD countries employment has declined during the 1975–78 period. These figures question the ability of the Western economies to solve their employment problems using purely neo-classical or Keynesian demand stimulation methods.

Figure 2.1 plots industrial output and employment in the nine EEC member countries during the period 1950–78. It can be seen that three very distinct patterns emerge:
- the period 1950–65, which is characterized by high growth in industrial output (7% annual average rate) accompanied by an important creation of employment (1% annual average growth rate);
- the period 1965–73, which is characterized by high growth in industrial output (6% annual average rate) and employment stagnation;
- the period 1973–78, characterized by low and stagnant growth in industrial output (1% annual average rate) accompanied by 'deployment' (−1.8% annual average rate).

Table 2.1. Production and Employment in Manufacturing Industry 1973-1978 (OECD) (1973 = 100)

OECD countries	Industrial output						Employment in industry					
	1973	1974	1975	1976	1977	1978*	1973	1974	1975	1976	1977	1978*
Canada	100	103.2	98.2	103.2	106.6	197.8	100	103.0	97.3	98.6	97.3	97.4
U.S.A.	100	99.6	90.8	100.0	105.6	110.9	100	99.9	91.4	94.5	97.4	100.8
Japan	100	96.2	86.0	95.5	99.5	10.49	100	99.4	94.1	91.6	90.0	87.5
Australia	100	102.6	94.8	100.0	98.3	100.0	100	100.5	92.9	94.5	88.9	86.6
Austria	100	105.0	98.5	104.7	108.3	110.4	100	99.6	94.5	93.0	93.8	92.6
Belgium	100	103.4	94.0	101.7	100.9	102.6	100	101.1	85.5	85.6	80.0	77.8
Denmark	100	95.7	89.6	100.0	100.9	107.8	100	95.6	85.4	86.3	84.4	81.9
Finland	100	105.0	100.8	101.7	98.3	102.5	100	105.0	104.3	100.5	99.0	96.7
France	100	102.5	95.0	103.3	105.0	105.8	100	100.8	98.2	97.1	96.4	92.5
Germany	100	98.6	93.0	99.8	102.8	102.7	100	97.3	90.8	88.6	88.8	88.3
Italy	100	103.9	94.8	105.8	105.8	108.4	100	104.0	104.2	103.0	97.0	95.5
The Netherlands	100	105.0	100.0	105.9	106.7	105.9	100	98.9	95.7	91.4	89.2	NA
Norway	100	104.3	111.3	119.1	120.0	101.7	100	100.8	105.7	106.9	105.1	100.8
Sweden	100	105.4	103.6	102.7	100.0	95.5	100	105.4	107.1	103.9	104.3	96.5
Switzerland	100	100.9	88.2	89.1	93.6	93.6	100	99.8	90.7	84.3	84.1	84.8
United Kingdom	100	98.2	92.8	93.7	95.5	97.3	100	100.5	95.7	92.6	93.9	93.7
Greece	100	98.4	102.7	113.6	115.9	123.1	100	100.9	101.7	108.5	112.8	113.7
Ireland	100	102.5	95.8	105.0	113.4	121.8	100	100.9	93.9	93.7	96.4	96.6
Spain	100	109.5	102.2	108.8	121.9	127.7	100	103.5	103.8	104.4	NA	NA
Yugoslavia	100	112.0	117.6	121.6	133.6	144.0	100	105.5	108.5	112.1	117.3	120.5

*First six months only.

Source: OECD (1976, 1978), UN (1978).

19

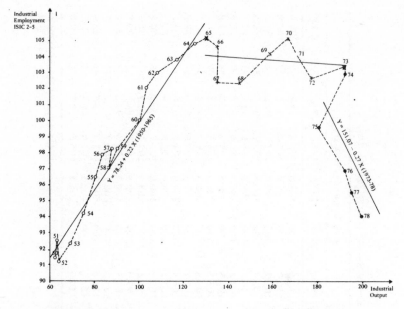

Source: EEC (1978), ILO (1977), OECD (1976, 1977, 1978), 1950–59 estimated

Figure 2.1. Industrial output and employment in the EEC-9 (1950–78): 1960 = 100.

Thus, since 1965 growth in industrial output has no longer been accompanied by a growth in employment; indeed, since 1973 the reverse has been the case within the EEC. Under these circumstances demand stimulation measures aimed at generating employment through growth in industrial output would seem to stand little chance of succeeding.

(b) *Structural change theory*

International competition explanation (1). If a significant percentage of employment in the labour-intensive industries in the Western economies has moved to the less developed, low wage cost countries (LDCs), then this might be expected to be reflected in a significant level of imports from the LDCs to the developed nations. Further, if this factor has grown in importance, and is making a major contribution to recent high levels

Table 2.2. *International Trade as a % of Domestic Consumption, Total Manufacture*

Trade as a % of domestic apparent consumption	U.K.		EEC-6		U.S.A.		Japan	
	1959–60	1973–74	1959–60	1973–74	1959–60	1973–74	1959–60	1973–74
External Imports	17.05	29.03	7.56	10.12	3.28	7.95	6.02	7.09
from LDCs	3.64	3.35	1.46	1.62	0.73	1.93	1.16	1.80
from DCs	12.41	24.42	5.53	7.53	2.53	5.66	4.74	4.61
External Exports	20.78	27.74	15.96	18.56	5.08	8.39	14.10	16.71

Table 2.3. *International Trade as a % of Domestic Consumption, Various Industries*

Trade as a % of domestic apparent consumption	U.K.		EEC-6		U.S.A.		Japan	
	1959-60	1973-74	1959-60	1973-74	1959-60	1973-74	1959-60	1973-74
1. Food, beverages								
External imports	32.71	29.21	4.67	4.98	2.73	4.28	4.41	6.84
from LDCs	7.61	5.46	2.06	1.63	1.29	1.69	3.08	2.20
from DCs	21.91	22.98	2.19	2.88	1.39	2.45	1.23	3.94
2. Textiles								
External imports	13.97	34.13	6.10	13.28	5.53	8.57	1.07	11.18
from LDCs	5.16	6.36	0.85	3.26	1.59	3.28	0.10	2.69
from DCs	8.29	26.11	4.94	8.60	3.94	4.95	0.96	7.14
3. Clothing								
External imports	9.48	26.77	2.38	11.45	3.47	14.31	1.42	16.81
from LDCs	3.91	10.33	0.56	4.15	0.77	6.19	0.71	8.50
from DCs	5.16	13.94	1.70	4.97	2.69	5.74	0.71	3.92
4. Wood, paper								
External imports	24.55	28.44	13.09	13.78	5.71	7.42	1.63	5.62
from LDCs	1.29	1.84	0.50	0.98	0.22	0.72	0.04	0.87
from DCs	20.64	24.33	11.47	11.60	5.48	6.47	1.60	4.19
5. Rubber								
External imports	2.09	7.54	2.79	4.13	1.15	4.20	0.46	1.51
from LDCs	0.14	0.17	0.06	0.11	0.02	0.16	0.02	0.30
from DCs	1.89	7.10	2.73	3.87	1.14	3.95	0.46	1.13
6. Chemicals								
External imports	16.13	34.23	14.47	16.17	2.44	6.28	10.81	13.84
from LDCs	2.85	3.44	2.73	2.50	0.64	1.14	0.41	1.34
from DCs	12.73	28.45	10.62	12.20	1.74	5.01	10.08	11.64

7. Petroleum products								
External imports	30.94	38.32	7.07	5.12	3.68	11.11	10.74	8.45
from LDCs	19.63	8.58	2.83	1.23	3.61	8.72	3.68	6.96
from DCs	10.95	28.80	2.26	1.84	0.07	2.16	6.81	0.99
8. Non-metal minerals								
External imports	3.23	8.05	2.18	3.02	2.03	3.68	0.61	0.83
from LDCs	0.03	0.10	0.03	0.06	0.10	0.36	0.00	0.14
from DCs	3.02	7.49	1.82	2.64	1.89	3.17	0.51	0.56
9. Ferrous and Non-ferrous								
External imports	23.35	40.81	14.50	17.38	6.04	12.51	17.85	18.90
from LDCs	6.63	6.69	5.01	5.29	0.97	2.11	4.30	6.69
from DCs	16.05	31.32	8.42	10.06	5.06	10.00	13.02	9.26
10. Transport equipment								
External imports	3.40	17.20	5.30	7.74	2.58	8.04	3.00	2.98
from LDCs	0.10	0.25	0.13	0.22	0.00	0.17	0.34	0.07
from DCs	3.29	16.61	5.07	7.22	2.57	7.80	2.66	2.90
11. Machinery and other								
External imports	10.39	32.53	7.23	11.52	2.25	8.65	6.06	5.19
from LDCs	0.77	1.56	0.09	0.44	0.07	1.43	0.04	0.43
from DCs	9.79	30.44	6.84	10.60	2.17	6.71	5.98	4.49

Source: UNCTAD (1978).

of unemployment, then the percentage of imports from the LDCs would be expected to be significantly higher today than, say, 20 or so years ago. Thus, by separating imports originating from LDCs from those originating from the advanced economies, it should be possible to separate international competition based largely on comparative advantage (i.e. low wage competition) and competition based largely on non-price factors (i.e. technical change).

Table 2.2 shows that international competition from developed countries is a more significant factor of domestic consumption — 4.31% (1959–60) to 7.35% (1973–74) — than international competition from LDCs (less than 2% of domestic consumption in the Western world) (Soete, 1978). Further, the evolution over time indicates that technical change international competition has grown more rapidly than low wage competition.

Other data, broken down for eleven broad industry groups, show that:
— In most industries foreign penetration of Western domestic markets is relatively high, and in the first place the result of competition from *developed* countries.

Above average penetration can be observed in textiles, clothing (except for the U.K.), chemicals (except for the U.S.A.), ferrous and non-ferrous metal products and machinery (except for Japan). Least subject to foreign competition are the food, rubber, non-metal mineral products and transport equipment industries.
— In terms of 'low wage' competition, market penetration is weak in all industrial sectors, except in clothing, petroleum products and ferrous and non-ferrous metal products (i.e. two natural resource intensive industries). Only in the food industry, textiles but also chemicals, do LDCs' imports represent more than 1% of domestic apparent consumption.
— In terms of growth, import competition has increased in all industrial sectors, especially in clothing (mainly low wage competition), but also in textiles, rubber, transport equipment and machinery. Growth has been lowest in the food and wood industries.

24

The natural conclusion to draw from the above figures is that, contrary to 'pure' trade theory, and the concept of the international division of labour, low-wage cost foreign competition has, directly, played only a minor part in the structural employment crisis in the Western economies. However, it might be that competition from low wage cost countries has accelerated the scrapping of old vintages, and also resulted in some product and process innovation, thereby having an indirect effect on structural change. What the figures in Table 2.2 do suggest, though, is that this process was due in the first place to increased competition from other developed economies and from increased market penetration. (2)

Thus, the unemployment aspect of technical change international competition is two-fold in its effect. In the first place jobs can be lost because of lack of competitiveness in the face of technically advanced imports. In the second place jobs are lost through rationalization by the home industry in attempting to increase its production efficiency to match that in major competitor countries (as well as, of course, attempting to overcome the price advantage enjoyed by traditional goods produced in the LDCs). In the long term it would seem that the unemployment impact of the former — that is lack of competitiveness because of technological backwardness in products — will be more significant than unemployment caused by rationalization of production facilities.

In order to verify in a more vigorous way the importance of technical change (continuous technical change between 1963 and 1976) on the export performance of all OECD countries (Iceland and New Zealand being excluded), Soete investigated the relationship between patents granted to those countries by the U.S. patents office between 1963 and 1976 in 40 industrial sectors, with (for all these OECD countries) the 1974 exports of the 40 industries. It was assumed in this analysis that the United States is the leading inventive activity country and market, and will thus attract most of the important patents from other OECD countries.

The results of this analysis are:

- for most capital goods industries, where a good deal of technical change is of the 'cost-reducing', continuous type, significant results are obtained;
- for most consumer goods — just as intermediate goods and materials, where technical change is weak and often of a very different nature — where cost-reducing technical change is more based on the diffusion of innovations that have occurred in the capital goods sector, non-significant results were obtained.

So, while technical change *per se* is important to competitiveness, from the analysis it seems that cost-reducing technical change in particular is also a crucial factor in international competition. Thus, in the Western economies, between 1963 and 1976, competition mainly from other developed countries has been the crucial factor in inducing industries into, in the first instance, job-displacing, labour-saving technical change.

The analysis above strongly suggests that innovation of a continuous, incremental type has had a significant impact on employment in the Western economies. Because of the relatively short time period covered, however, (1963–76) this in no way precludes the Schumpeterian interpretation based on 'clusters' of important innovations. In fact, the data in Figure 2.1 might be taken to support Schumpeter's theory. The next section deals with the 'wave-theory' of innovation and structural unemployment in some detail.

(iv) Long waves, technical change and employment*

Long-wave theory. During the 1920s Kondratiev attempted to collect statistical evidence for the existence of 'long waves' in the world economy, and to provide a theoretical explanation for them. These long waves — the so-called Kondratiev waves — lasted for between 50 and 60 years. Kondratiev explained them primarily in terms of the durability of certain types of invest-

---

*For a detailed analysis of this topic, see C. Freeman (1977).

ment such as buildings and transport, changes in the price level and fluctuations in savings and availability of credit. While he did suggest that when a major wave of expansion was under way inventions that had lain dormant would find application, he did not explicitly discuss the nature and direction of technical change.

Schumpeter (1939) later took up the notion of long waves and introduced the idea of technological revolutions as the driving force of the Kondratiev cycles: he pointed in particular to the role of steam power in the first Kondratiev (1787–1842), of railroads in the second Kondratiev (1843–97) and of electric power and the automobile in the third Kondratiev; he related these major changes primarily to bursts of creative activity by entrepreneurs. As Kuznets (1940) pointed out, however, there is no special reason to expect that the intensity of entrepreneurial innovative activity will vary in this manner, i.e. in long cycles. Kuznets did accept the possibility of a bunching of innovations associated with new technologies and of investment activities associated with these waves of innovation. Such bunches of innovations would need to be such that their effects would permeate throughout the economic system and be far reaching.

Glismann, Rodemar and Wolter (1978) have collected data which appear to offer some justification of the claim for the existence of long waves in the growth of the German economy. The expansionary phase of these long waves is characterized by a more rapid growth of production, a higher rate of growth of international trade and relatively high levels of employment compared with the down-swings. The periods of high growth include booms and periods of 'recession' or faltering growth; the periods of no growth or stagnation include depression and revival from depression.

More recently Mensch (1978) has mapped the last 200 years of technico-economic history and has identified a clustering of *basic* innovations around the years 1770, 1825, 1885 and 1935. Mensch disclaimed a direct connection with Kondratiev-type long waves, but comparison of his innovation clusters with

27

Kondratiev's waves is nevertheless interesting (Ray, 1979).

While time series on unemployment are lacking for the nineteenth century, and the evidence of the twentieth century is not satisfactory, nevertheless, as Freeman puts it, '. . . there can be little doubt that the period from 1918 to 1939 was one of much higher levels of unemployment than the quarter-centuries which preceded the First World War or followed the Second World War. Nor again is there much doubt that the inter-war period was one of relative stagnation in the growth of trade and output, compared with the periods which preceded and followed it. It is hardly surprising that many people are now asking if there is any evidence to support the hypothesis that the last quarter of the twentieth century may tend to resemble the second more than the third, unless international economic policies are adjusted to avoid this outcome' (Freeman, 1977).

Technical change and the Kondratiev. As we have seen earlier in this book not all technical change is employment generating. It might be that in the early stages, following the Schumpeterian bunching of major innovations, there is an increase in investment accompanied by the creation of new industries producing new products and processes, and generating many new employment opportunities. As the industries mature, the nature of innovation changes towards a regime of standardization and cost-reduction, with a resultant fall in employment as more and more labour-saving devices and techniques are introduced into the production process. Because of the absence of major new technological opportunities in the Kondratiev down-swings, a general climate of stagnation and recession would be made more severe by this technology-led employment displacement, leading eventually to severe depression.

A scheme of the sort of pattern of change over time following the introduction of a major new technology, which might give rise to swings in the level of employment associated with a Kondratiev wave, has been devised by Freeman (1977), and is shown in Table 2.4.

Freeman's scheme emphasizes Schumpeter's observation that

the major new technologies were already in use on a small scale in the preceding Kondratiev cycle. For example, the railways were established on a small scale before the second Kondratiev, and the electrical and automobile industries were similarly established before the third Kondratiev. A major new technology requires a whole cluster of related inventions, innovations and institutional changes before it can begin to have a major economic impact. It is for this reason that Freeman's first column (Table 2.4) represents the down-swing phase of the Kondratiev which precedes the boom of the 'carrier' Kondratiev.

Technical change and the electronics industry. Freeman (1977) described the growth of the electronics* industry as a possible example of the pattern outlined in Table 2.4; in particular, he considered the electronics capital goods industry and the components industry:

> The computer is the most revolutionary new development to emerge from the Second World War. Through the use of electronics technology computers and calculators became much faster and more reliable. Even the first electronic computers were over 1,000 times faster than electro-mechanical computers. They could find application in almost every other manufacturing and service activity in the industrialized economies. This is exactly the type of major new technology which might be expected to exemplify the modified Kondratiev pattern which we have postulated. Automation is of course possible without computers. . . . But the speed, reliability and power of the computer have vastly and rapidly extended the possibilities of automation. . . . Automation takes mechanization an enormous step further since it reduces the labour requirements for operating, setting, controlling and maintaining machines in addition to the simple handling and transfer of materials, components and equipment.

*As Freeman points out, the radio industry, the precursor of the modern electronics industry, was well established during the previous Kondratiev cycle.

29

Table 2.4. *A Simplified Schematic Representation of the Introduction of Major New Technologies*

	Previous Kondratiev	'Main carrier' Kondratiev		Subsequent Kondratiev
		Upswing	Downswing	
Research invention	Basic science coupled to technical exploitation. Key patents, many prototypes.	Intensive applied R & D for new products and applications, and for back-up to trouble shooting from production experience.	Continuing high level of research and inventive activity with emphasis shifting to cost-saving.	
Design	Imaginative leaps. Rapid changes. No standardization, competing design philosophies. Some disasters.	Still big new developments but increasing role of standardization and regulation.	Technical change still rapid but increasing emphasis on cost and standard components.	Settling down to routine 'model' type changes and minor improvements of cumulative importance.
Production	One-off experimental and moving to small batch. Close link with R & D and design. Negligible scale economies.	Move to larger batches and where applicable flow processes and mass production. Economies of scale begin to be important.	Major economies of scale affecting labour and capital but especially labour. Larger firms and establishments.	Continued growth of output and productivity.
Investment	High risk speculative, small scale. Some inventor-entrepreneurs. Some large firms. Fairly labour-intensive.	Band-wagon. Large and small firms attracted by high growth and high profits and new opportunities.	Continuing rapid growth, but increasingly large sums required to finance R & D and rising capital costs. Rising capital intensity.	

Market structure and demand	Innovator monopolies. Strong consumer resistance and ignorance.	Intense technological competition for better design and performance. Falling prices. Big fashion effects.	Growing concentration. Intense technological competition and some price competition. Strong pressure to export and exploit scale economies.	Trend to oligopoly or monopoly structure. Bankruptcies and mergers.
Labour	Small-scale employment generating effects. High proportion of skilled labour, engineers and technicians. Training and learning on the job and in R & D.	Major employment generating effects as production expands. New training and education facilities set up and expand rapidly. New skills in short supply. Rapid increase in pay.	Employment growth slows down, and as capital intensity rises, some jobs become increasingly routine. Skilled labour supply catches up with demand.	Employment level still expanding slowly, but main emphasis on maintaining output with same labour force. Later, the labour force may decline in absolute terms.
Employment effects on other industries and services.	Negligible, but imaginative engineers, managers and inventors are thinking about them and investing accordingly.	Substantial secondary effects, mainly employment generating initially but gradually swinging to displacement.	Major labour displacement effects, as new technology now firmly established and strongly cost-reducing.	Continuing labour displacement as new technology penetrates remaining industries and services.

Employment in the computer industry itself, although of course it grew very rapidly in the 1950's and 1960's, is not actually very big. In the United States it is only just over 200,000. The really important employment effects are outside the industry itself . . . it is estimated that at least ten times as many people, i.e. about 2-million, are working on computer installations, in computer bureaux, and various types of computer service activity. This employment is very widely distributed throughout the economy, as almost every large firm, government organization and university now has its own computer facility, with its associated personnel. There are now over 100,000 such data-processing installations in the United States and there will probably soon be as many in Europe. Computers were sometimes sold to customers on the basis that they would 'save' labour by eliminating routine clerical and 'number-crunching' activities. In some cases they may have had this effect, but the evidence which it has been possible to assemble suggests that in the vast majority of cases, the first effect of installing a computer was to add to existing employment not to reduce it. Labour-displacing effects may have followed, but almost always with considerable delays. Since almost all computers now in operation were only installed since 1960, any effects of this kind are probably still to come, at least for Europe and Japan.

Total employment in the United States electronics industry grew from 56,000 in 1939 to 350,000 in 1950. It reached its peak in 1969 at 1,254,000. Since then, it has fluctuated a little around a slight downward trend and in 1975 stood at 1,115,000. Precisely comparable European figures are not available but employment followed a similar growth with some lags and has now levelled off, as in the United States. . . . There is no doubt that labour productivity has been increasing rapidly and continued to increase after employment levelled off.

All through the 1950's, the pace of technical change was extremely rapid in the electronics capital goods, and component industries. They were highly labour-intensive and the barriers to entry were mainly technological. The new firms which attempted to enter the industry were a mixture of large electric and office equipment firms with strong R & D and technical resources, and small 'spin-off' firms, established by break-away groups of technologists with up-to-date knowledge of technical possibilities. But during the 1960's the mortality rate was high, both among large and small new entrants, and a process of concentration was evident. Economies of scale became very important in R & D, design, manufacture and marketing. . . . Capital-intensity increased, and the pace of technical change remained fast enough to deter all but the most determined new entrants. The structure of the industry began to settle down with a few very powerful US-based multi-nationals. . . .

As Freeman points out, the later development and application of large-scale integrated circuits (LSIs) has had even more revolutionary consequences than the development of the transistor. There has been a drastic fall in the cost of microprocessors, and this means that the competitive substitution pressure in a wide range of industries and services will become increasingly intense in the last quarter of the twentieth century. Indeed, this has already occurred with devastating consequences in the mechanical precision watch industry (Chapter 6 (i)).

The LSI chip will undoubtedly, because it replaces a number of separate components or circuits, reduce employment in component manufacture. Its major impact on employment, however, will occur outside the electronics industry. Freeman cites two examples of this: the cash register and telephone equipment industries.

According to the 1975 Annual Report of National Cash Register, the world's leading manufacturer:

We can now produce . . . microcircuits, not much bigger than the head of a pin, which contain up to 16,000 components. These replace mechanisms that required hundreds of individually mechanised parts and scores of space-consuming machine tools and manufacturing processes to produce them.

33

As a result of this, over a five-year period, total employment at NCR has fallen from about 100,000 to 70,000. The fall in manufacturing employment has been more than 50% (37,000 in 1970 to 18,000 in 1975) during the same period. At the same time, revenue per employee has doubled and R & D costs have quadrupled.

In Western Electric — the manufacturing arm for ATT — employment in the switching equipment division fell, as the result of the shift from electromechanical to electronics technology, from 39,200 direct employees in 1970 to 19,000 in 1976. By 1980 this is expected to fall to 17,400. Indirect labour is expected to fall similarly, although this will be marginally compensated by an increase of about 600 in the number working on software. Further, there will be a drastic reduction in employment on fault finding, maintenance and repair, and Western Electric estimates that the installation work force will be reduced by 75%.

Similar effects are occurring (although more slowly) in Western Europe, and in the United Kingdom employment fell between 1973 and 1978 by as much as 30% (see Chapter 6 (iv)).

Now, while the post-Second World War changes in the electronics industry, outlined above, do not exactly replicate the scheme outlined in Table 2.3, nevertheless the pattern is suggestive of a Kondratiev-type cycle. The similarities are sufficient to suggest that Freeman's scheme provides a useful analytical framework for interpreting long-term relationships between technical change and changes in employment in industries undergoing major changes in technology and manufacturing techniques.

References

1. Aubert (1978) has commented on the role that lack of international competitiveness has played in creating unemployment in France. He points to the emphasis in France on mass production using relatively unskilled labour. (Of employment generated in France between 1961–70 in firms employing more than 100, over 50% of jobs were created in firms employing the least qualified manpower — also, two-thirds of the 350,000 jobs created in industry between 1968 and 1975 were

34

filled by immigrant (unskilled) workers.) This has led to a disregard for quality and variety and 'for maintaining the technological and industrial heritage'. As a result, 'The traditional industries are coming apart at the seams:

- productivity gains in heavy industry, particularly iron and steel, have been negligible compared to those of competitors; there has been scant diversification and the few attempts (special steels) have floundered; the massive assistance misguidedly provided by the authorities and the banks have only served to conceal their disintegration and temporarily stave off inevitable conversion;
- the traditional industries (leather, textiles, wood, furniture, etc.) have failed to upgrade their products and modernize their plant and are losing jobs on a substantial scale; the process is far from over (30% of the jobs in the textile industry are due to disappear by 1985 due solely to competition from developing countries)'.

Thus, Aubert sees lack of international competitiveness as a major cause of job loss in France. Jobs are lost mainly, as Soete said, in some areas through lack of product innovation and variety, and in others through a failure to up-date traditional production sequences (e.g. in textiles) to meet low wage cost competition from LDCs.

2. Rothwell (1978) has investigated the relationship between 'technical quality' and international competitiveness in engineering goods produced in the U.K. and West Germany. This analysis showed that competitiveness was a function of product quality and that low quality was associated with high import penetration. It provides strong support for the 'technical change' international competitiveness theory.

CHAPTER 3

STRUCTURAL CHANGES IN POST-WAR PATTERNS OF EMPLOYMENT

(i) Patterns of employment

Figure 3.1 shows the pattern of employment change in seven OECD member countries between 1955 and 1975. It shows that in all these countries the proportion of the workforce employed in agriculture has fallen. The pattern of change in manufacturing employment is less consistent, with Japan and France showing an initial growth. This might, however, be due to both these countries initially having relatively high agricultural employment proportions. The proportion of the workforce in service employment has grown fairly consistently in all seven countries.*

Figure 3.2 shows the rates of growth of employment in manufacturing, commerce, other services and agriculture between 1953 and 1973 in six OECD member countries. Despite some variations between countries, and some peculiarities in the direction and rate of change of employment growth over time, it can be seen that the rate of increase in manufacturing employment — which had been generally high in the 1950s — had slowed down markedly in nearly all cases well before the 1973/4 slump. It also shows fairly consistent positive growth rates in the service sectors.

---

*The service sector includes both consumer and producer services. For example, in the U.K. in 1975, of the 45% of the workforce employed in the service sector, 22% were in consumer services and 23% in the producer services.

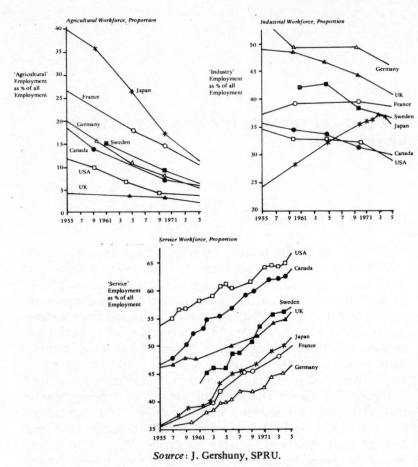

Source: J. Gershuny, SPRU.

Figure 3.1. Sectoral employment in the seven economies.

(ii) Jobless growth

Most OECD countries have experienced an absolute decline in employment in manufacturing since 1973. The fact that this decline had begun in some countries before 1973, linked to the slowing down in the growth of manufacturing employment in the 1960s, suggests that it is part of a long-term structural change in the pattern of output and employment.

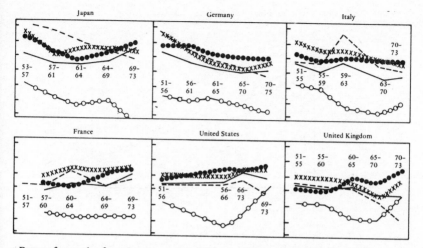

Rates of growth of employment are as follows: overall ——, in manufacturing ‑‑‑; in commerce xxxxx; in other services ●●and, in agriculture o—o. For 1970–73 it was necessary to use the rate of growth of employment in commerce and other services.
Sources: Cripps and Tarling, op. cit.; and *Labour Force Statistics, 1962–1973*, op. cit. Reproduced from: Cornwall, *Modern Capitalism*, Martin Robertson, Oxford, 1978.

Figure 3.2. Rates of growth of employment by activities.

Now, it is well known that a pattern of 'jobless' output has been established in the agriculture sector for a long time, i.e. that the decline in agricultural employment has generally been accompanied by a rise in agricultural output (and a fairly rapid increase in the capital intensity of agriculture). This is shown for the U.K. in Figure 3.3. Figure 3.4 shows industrial manpower productivity in the seven OECD member countries covered by Figure 3.1 during the period 1955–75: productivity in all cases underwent fairly consistent growth.* These data, linked to Figure 2.1, suggest that a pattern of jobless growth is being established in some advanced economies in the

*According to Gershuny (1979), the temporary reversal in labour productivity growth after 1973 was largely due to government-financed job maintenance schemes and employment protection laws which in the slump combined to produce 'disguised unemployment'.

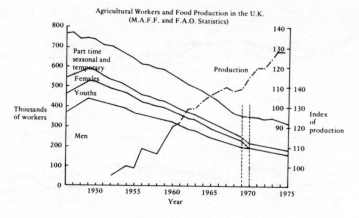

Agricultural Workers and Food Production in the U.K.
(M.A.F.F. and F.A.O. Statistics)

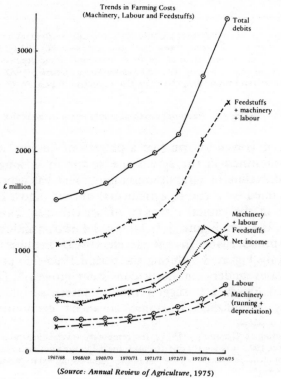

Trends in Farming Costs
(Machinery, Labour and Feedstuffs)

(*Source: Annual Review of Agriculture*, 1975)

Figure 3.3

40

manufacturing sector. Based on our earlier discussion (Chapter 2), it seems reasonable to suggest that the prime mover in establishing this pattern is rationalization of production sequences. According to Cox (1978) this process accelerated in a number of countries during the 1970s as a result of high wage cost inflation which made investment in labour-saving plant more attractive. (1)

(iii) The role of the service sector

It has been argued above that the pattern of jobless growth, which has been long characteristic of the agriculture sector, is becoming established in manufacturing industry in the advanced economies. As the data showed, during the past 30 years or so most of the 'excess' employment has been taken up in the fast growing service sector. The question is, will employment in the tertiary sector continue to expand, and if so, at a sufficient pace to accommodate the labour released through structural change in manufacturing?

It might first be useful, before attempting to answer the above question, to try to explain why employment in the service sector has grown so much more rapidly than in manufacturing industry. Fuchs (1968) examined patterns of employment change in the United States over the period 1929–65. He suggested four possible reasons for the more rapid growth of employment in services there:

— The *quality* of labour increased faster in industry than in service activities: 'of all the variables identified, labour quality is probably the most important one in explaining the differential trend in employment'.
— Hours of work declined faster in service industries and institutions than in goods-producing industries.
— Capital per worker increased faster in goods producing industries than in service activities.
— Goods-producing industries have experienced a faster rate of technological change than service industries and institutions.

41

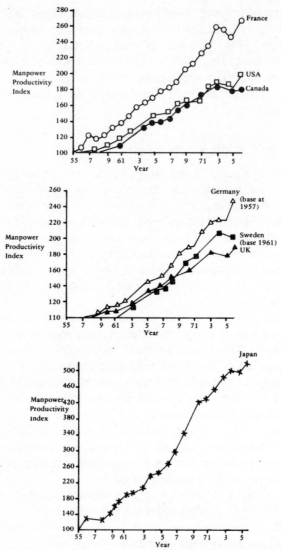

The figures for the OECD as a whole show very little variation from year to year.

Figure 3.4a. Industrial manpower productivity in the seven economies.

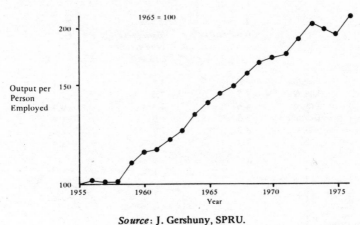

Source: J. Gershuny, SPRU.

Figure 3.4b. OECD Industrial Manpower Productivity Index.

Now, while it is generally recognized that the marked shift of employment to the service sector is related to the increase in demand for commercial and public services by consumers and businesses, nevertheless the slow growth in labour productivity in this sector made a major·contribution to this shift.

Gershuny (1979) also discusses this shift in terms of differences in labour productivity between the secondary and tertiary sectors:

> One condition for maintenance of full employment in an economy (holding relative wages constant) must be that the total product rises at the same rate as does the average manpower productivity across the economy. Over the past two decades, throughout the OECD, manpower productivity in manufacturing industry has risen faster than GNP [Figure 3.5]. Employment can only be maintained under such conditions by passing labour into the relatively low productivity, low productivity growth, service sector.

This again raises the question of the future ability of the service sector to continue to generate large numbers of jobs. In

43

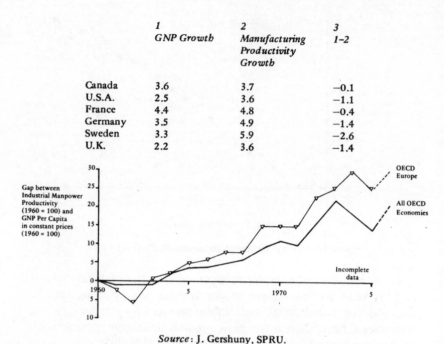

	1 GNP Growth	2 Manufacturing Productivity Growth	3 1–2
Canada	3.6	3.7	−0.1
U.S.A.	2.5	3.6	−1.1
France	4.4	4.8	−0.4
Germany	3.5	4.9	−1.4
Sweden	3.3	5.9	−2.6
U.K.	2.2	3.6	−1.4

Source: J. Gershuny, SPRU.

Figure 3.5. Gap between manufacturing productivity growth and GNP Growth, 1960–74.

attempting to answer this question, Peitchinis (1978) looked at current trends in the four variables identified by Fuchs:

In relation to the quality of labour, the general level of education increased substantially over the past two decades. To the extent that quality is measured in terms of the average level of education possessed by the labour force, it is doubtful that there remains any difference on the average between the level of those in goods-producing industries and the level of those in service industries and institutions. Indeed, considering the very substantial increase in the numbers of teachers, nurses, all categories of professionals, public service administrators and scores of other high quality occupations over the past two decades, it is conceivable that the average level of education of the labour force engaged in service activities now exceeds the average level of those engaged in goods-producing activities.

Regarding the hours of work in services and industry, statistical evidence suggests that while the standard hours are still lower in service industries and institutions than in goods-producing industries, the gap is not as wide on the average as it was ten or more years ago. The evidence suggests perhaps that the standard hours of work in service activities reached a level of downward resistance, whereas those prevailing in goods-producing industries are still at levels which have downward flexibility.

In relation to the third variable, i.e. capital investment, service industries have lagged substantially behind goods-producing industries *on the average*,* largely because of a lack of appropriate technology.† In recent years some significant changes have been recorded: the advent of electronic data processing has been rapidly transforming labour intensive processes into capital intensive electronic processes; as a result, substantial increases in capital investment are being recorded in service industries and institutions, as well as in the service areas of goods-producing industries, such as marketing, warehousing, planning, finance, and other office and administrative activity areas.

In relation to the fourth variable, i.e. the rate of technology change, it is not surprising that goods-producing industries should have recorded a faster rate than service industries, since in many service activities there has been relatively limited deployment of technology. But, significant changes have been recorded in recent years: the transformation of labour intensive processes into electronic processes

---

*In certain industries of the service sector, such as Utilities and Transportation, capital investment per employed worker is considerably higher than that of industries in the goods-producing sector.

†The capital investment to which reference is made here relates to investment in capital goods. It does not take into account investment in human capital, which is very substantial in occupations employed in the service sector.

has been accompanied by an acceleration in the rate of technological change.

Now if the more rapid growth of employment in the tertiary sector can be explained largely by the four variables forwarded by Fuchs (lower quality of labour, shorter working week, lower *per capita* capital investment, slower rate of technological change), then the significant recent improvements in all these variables described by Peitchinis can be expected to reduce the future rate of growth in employment. As Peitchinis puts it:

> The question now arises whether the widespread application of electronic technology in service activities will reduce the rate of increase in employment in the (service) sector in the way that mechanical technology reduced the rate of increase in employment in goods-producing processes. There is no apparent reason for the employment effects of technology to be different in service activities from those in goods-producing activities.

In relation to this crucial point, Peitchinis goes on to state:

> Heretofore, changes in technology entailed, for the most part, increases in the speed of equipment and improvements in materials. In most activities, particularly in the service sector, the worker–machine ratio remained unchanged. For example, scores of improvements have been introduced to the typewriter and to activities and materials related to the typing function (paper, erasers etc.), but the typist–typewriter ratio remained unchanged — the operation of each typewriter required a typist. To the extent that the increase in speed in typing activity could not satisfy the increase in demand for typing services, and more typewriters had to be added, for each additional typewriter a typist had to be employed. This provides a basic general explanation for the rapid increase of employment in the service sector: demand

for services increased faster than the increase of productivity in the sector.

The application of electronic technology to service sector processes facilitates a change in the worker–machine ratio that was not possible to the same extent under mechanical technology: a number of typewriters can now be linked to a computer and can perform the typing function without the participation of typists. The need for another typewriter does not generate demand for another typist. This capacity to link production processes to electronic systems, and thereby reduce the worker–machine ratio, has very significant implications for the future labour absorptive capacity of the service sector, and that of the economy at large. Developed economies are confronted with a critical problem.

(iv) The public and private service sectors

So far the tertiary sector has been treated as if it was fairly homogenous. The distinction must be made, however, between the public service sector and the private service sector, and Freeman (1978) sees this distinction as crucial in explaining the success of the U.S. government in generating millions of new jobs in the tertiary sector between 1975 and 1978.

A high proportion of these new jobs were generated in the public sector, partly as a direct result of various job creation schemes and partly from continuing expansion of education and welfare activities, especially at the State level (as opposed to Federal). This has also been a common experience in Europe in the recent past with health service, education and various forms of environmental services undergoing rapid expansion.

But what about the future growth of public sector employment? During recent years pressure for *wage parity* in this (highly labour-intensive) sector has been a major source of wage cost inflation; and it has generated problems of the scale and control of public expenditure where these services are financed primarily through government budgets and taxes, both central and local. This has led to widespread political pressure to resist further increases in taxation and increases in public expenditure on service activities and thus employment (an example being proposition 13 of a recent Californian referendum). Too high taxation can also be seen to lead to growth in a 'black economy'. Government counter-inflationary policies in both Europe and the U.S.A. are also aimed at reducing budget deficits and curbing public expenditure. Future expansion in public sector activities on a scale experienced in the past would thus seem unlikely.

In view of the above, it seems likely that the main hopes for future service employment growth must lie in the expansion of the private service sector, and if aggregate demand is raised sufficiently, then this must surely exert a demand for goods and services somewhere in the economic system, with a growth in jobs to provide these extra goods and services. But is this necessarily true? And if so, how great will be the job creation effects of increased demand? As was seen earlier, in the manufacturing sector more goods can be produced with little if any increase in labour via investment in labour-saving equipment. Moreover, recent developments in electronics technology promise to make it possible to increase output in some parts of the service sector (e.g. offices, banking) without a correspondingly large increase in labour. If, as Peitchinis has suggested, current trends allow for a greatly increased improvement in service sector productivity, then much of the increase in aggregate demand might be met with very little increase in private service sector employment.

(v) Producer services and consumer services

Finally, in this section, it is worth while making the distinction between 'producer services' — those service industries whose products are an intermediate input to the final production of material goods — and 'consumer services' — industries providing services for final consumption.

Gershuny (1979) has made a study of factors — technical and otherwise — having an impact on employment in these sub-sectors of the consumer industry:

Technical advances increasingly promote dramatic increases in manpower productivity in this part of the service sector (producer services); routine or repetitive technical and clerical jobs are progressively replaced by machines. In banking and insurance, the management of accounts by large data processing systems is already virtually universal. In the retail trade, computerised stock management and automatic retail checkout systems are both well established and still growing. In the technical services sector, computerised design systems are increasingly substituted for a wide range of processes which previously required highly skilled human labour. And there is good reason for supposing that the skilled jobs generated by the process of automation will not compensate for the jobs lost as a result of automation — the purpose is, after all, the saving of labour costs.

So, if new jobs are to be found at all, it must be in the provision of final services: there is, however, good reason for supposing that growth in 'consumer services' industries may be restrained in the future. There are grounds for suggesting that future provision of services in developed countries may be increasingly extra-economic, that jobs in service industries may be replaced by activities undertaken within households or by other sorts of voluntary associations outside the money economy. This process has already been seen over recent decades in a number of service industries. The transport service sector, for example, has diminished considerably, since people no longer *buy* the final service from railway or bus systems, but instead *buy* cars, and *produce the final service themselves.* Similarly, domestic tasks once carried out by paid servants in middle-class homes are now carried out by the householders themselves using domestic machinery. And entertainment, once provided

49

largely in the form of services purchased and consumed out of the home, is now produced 'informally' within the household, using goods purchased from the formal 'money' economy.

As increasingly sophisticated design makes the use of consumer goods easier, and improves the quality of their output, and as organizational and technical change in the manufacturing sector make their production cheaper, the movement away from purchasing 'services' and toward 'self-service' (via the purchase of goods) is likely to accelerate. (With recent technological advances the spread in self-service activities also seems likely to increase into such *public* service fields as education and medicine.) Thus, the scope for the future expansion in employment in both the producer and consumer parts of the private service sector would appear to be limited, and this reduction in employment growth rate seems largely due to technical change.

References

1. Cox (1978) has presented extremely convincing data from the United Kingdom and West Germany mechanical engineering industries to show that where there is a mis-match between sales receipts and employment costs, firms shed labour and rationalization investment replaces growth or replacement investment. The process of employment loss through wage cost inflation is illustrated in the table below:

Rise in value of sales receipts and cost per employee, and employment changes

	Percentage increase per year		Actual change in employment
	Costs per employee %	Sales %	
United Kingdom			
1958 to 1963	3	6	+56,000
1963 to 1967	7	9	+33,000
1967 to 1971	12	14	+54,000
1971 to 1975	23	19	−73,000

(continued)

| | Percentage increase per year | | Actual change in employment |
	Costs per employee %	Sales %	
West Germany			
1967 to 1971	15	16	+143,900
1971 to 1975	9	7	−96,100

Cox concludes: '. . . in current output technological development is responsible for maintaining and increasing sales and, potentially, the numbers employed. If however unions negotiate an average cost per employee that is out of line with increase in sales receipts, then technical development comes to play an additional role — that of substituting machine effort for human effort, which has become too expensive.' Thus, wage- and social security-push have reduced employment and favoured rationalization investment.

CHAPTER 4

PATTERNS OF UNEMPLOYMENT

At the outset it is important to note that unemployment is extremely difficult to compare accurately across countries because of different definitions and different social and training schemes which mask true levels of employment.

(i) Quantitative changes

Table 4.1 shows unemployment as a percentage of the labour force in sixteen OECD member countries for the years 1973 to 1978. Considering only the *rich* OECD members, it can be seen that there are basically three patterns in unemployment trends: (1) those nations which, despite the 1974 slump, succeeded in maintaining relatively low levels of unemployment (Japan and Sweden); (2) those nations in which unemployment rose sharply in 1975, and where it has subsequently remained high or increased (Italy, U.K., France, Netherlands, Belgium, West Germany); (3) those nations in which unemployment rose sharply in 1975, and where it has subsequently decreased to near 1974 levels (U.S.A.).

For various reasons, Japan might be treated as a special case.

In the case of Sweden, the successful maintenance of low levels of unemployment might be ascribed to a number of causes:

— a traditional state of accord between government, labour and management has enabled adjustment to take place via retrain-

Table 4.1. *Levels of Unemployment* (1) *(percentage of labour force)*

	1962–73 (average)	1974	1975	1976	1977	1978 (2)
Canada	5.3	5.4	7.1	7.2	8.1	8.4
U.S.A.	4.9	5.6	8.5	7.7	7.0	6.0
Japan	1.3	1.4	1.9	2.0	2.0	2.2
Australia	1.6	2.3	4.4	4.4	5.6	6.4
Belgium	2.1	2.6	4.5	5.8	6.6	7.1
Denmark		2.5	6.0	6.1	7.7	8.5
Finland	2.4	1.7	2.2	4.0	6.1	6.7
France	1.8	2.3	4.0	4.2	4.8	4.8
German F.R.	1.3	2.7	4.8	4.7	4.6	4.3
Italy	3.6	2.9	3.3	3.7	7.2 (3)	6.9
Netherlands	1.4	3.3	4.7	5.1	4.9	5.0
Norway	0.9	0.6	1.2	1.1	0.9	1.0
Spain		2.2	3.8	4.9	5.7	7.0
Sweden	2.1	2.0	1.6	1.6	1.8	2.2
U.K.	2.4	2.5	3.9	5.4	5.7	5.7
Ireland		7.9	12.2	12.3	11.9	11.8

(1) National definitions, not adjusted for international comparability.
(2) 1978: latest 3 months available (usually second quarter).
(3) New survey definitions, not comparable with previous years.
Source: OECD 'Economic Outlook' and 'Selected Economic Indicators'.

ing and relocation schemes. In this way, large numbers of workers have been successfully shifted from agriculture — mainly forestry work — into manufacturing industry;
- under this tripartite system of co-operation, willingness to be retrained has been linked to social security benefits;
- Sweden, despite relatively high wage costs, has been successfully competitive in international markets with the production of high value added, sophisticated goods;
- employment protection legislation has made it difficult for Swedish companies to shed labour during times of recession.

In Western Europe, while a slow down in economic growth, and hence demand, during and after the 1974/5 recession has undoubtedly had a detrimental impact on employment, recent studies have emphasized the influence of *structural* factors. In the older industrial countries, the pattern of new investment in manufacturing industry has shifted markedly into cost-saving rationalization rather than new capacity extension.

In Western Europe there are basically two models:

(a) Successfully competitive countries. The prime example of this is West Germany which, via the efficient production of high quality goods — notably in the engineering sectors — has maintained a relatively large share of OECD trade as well as vigorously expanding into non-OECD market areas.* As the figures in Table 4.1 show, unemployment levels in West Germany have fallen consistently, if only marginally, since 1975.

(b) Less successful competitors. An example of this is the U.K., which has suffered a decline in share of OECD trade. Here the unemployment level increased after 1975, and has remained high.

In the successfully competitive countries enjoying a large trade surplus, it might be possible to soak up structural unemployment by expanding education, health care, public works, etc., and by investing some of the surplus in new industries. In the less successful countries, the ability to expand public service sectors is very much reduced without significant increases in taxation. Indeed, the public health sector in the U.K. already appears to be in a state of decline through cash shortages.

It might be, as in Sweden, that employment protection legislation has prevented unemployment levels from rising even higher in some Western European countries. There is evidence to suggest, however, that employment protection laws in several European countries have reduced the inclination of some companies to hire labour and have actively encouraged them to seek increased output via rationalization of production sequences.

The U.S.A. is the only major trading nation which has succeeded in significantly reducing its level of unemployment between 1975 and 1978 (which has supported the belief of U.S.

---

*In 1971 and 1975, West Germany's percentages of exports of engineering products to non-OECD countries were 24.1% and 34.7% respectively. During both these years West Germany enjoyed a 22% share of OECD markets in engineering goods.

economists in aggregate demand theory). As was seen in Chapter 3 of this book, this is partially due to the success of government measures in generating new jobs in the public sector. There might additionally be a more fundamental reason which relates to the *structure* of U.S. industry.

A recent report commissioned by the Anglo-German Foundation showed that new technology-based firms have played a major role in the U.S. economy, while their role in the U.K. and West Germany has been only small (A. D. Little Ltd., 1977).* Trade statistics also show that U.S. exports are more technology intensive than those from other major OECD exporters (Table 4.2). Now, it is well known that the U.S. led

Table 4.2. *OECD Exports of Manufacturers, 1968 and 1974: Composition of Exports (technology-intensive, non technology-intensive), Percentage*

	OECD	U.S.	Japan	France	Germany	U.K.
1968						
Technology-intensive	28.4	40.5	26.0	26.0	26.2	30.5
Non technology-intensive	71.6	59.5	74.0	74.0	73.8	69.5
1974						
Technology-intensive	29.9	42.5	27.0	26.7	28.9	31.8
Non technology-intensive	70.1	57.5	72.8	73.3	71.1	68.2

Source: R. Kelly, 'The Impact of Technological Innovations on International Trade Patterns', *Technological Innovation: A Government/Industry Co-operative Effort*, ed. A. Gersterfeld, John Wiley & Sons, New York, 1978.

the world in the production of semiconductor and semiconductor devices. A similar pattern is being established in the production of microelectronic circuits and devices. In both instances initially small, but fast-growing high-technology firms played a major role in the production of these new technologies and devices. It might be, therefore, that the recent development of

---

*There are several thousand NTBFs in the U.S. employing in excess of 2 million. In the Silicon Valley area alone, in 1974 there were 800 NTBFs with annual sales of $2.5 billion. In the U.K. the number of NTBFs currently in existence is only about 200 with total sales of £200 million. In West Germany the number of NTBFs is even less.

microelectronics in the U.S. has played an important role in the generation of new jobs via the creation of many new, fast-growing high-technology firms. (Between 1963 and 1973, the growth of the U.S. semiconductor industry was five times that of the U.S. GNP; growth of the integrated circuit segment was about eighty times that of the U.S. GNP.)

The results of a recent study by the U.S. Department of Commerce would appear to lend some support to this 'new small firm' argument (NSF, 1978). The study looked at six 'mature' corporations (including General Motors and Bethlehem Steel), five 'innovative' companies (including Polaroid and IBM) and five 'young high-technology' firms (such as Marion Labs. and Digital Equipment). The mature firms, which had combined annual sales of $36 billion, added only 25,000 workers between 1973 and 1978; the innovative companies, with combined annual sales of $21 billion, added 106,000 workers; the high-technology companies, with total sales of $857 million, created 35,000 new jobs.*

In the 1950s and 1960s the semiconductor and computer hardware industries were generating a lot of new employment. In the 1970s the main growth in employment has not derived from the hardware side, but from the software side, e.g. computer bureaux, information services, where new small firms have proliferated.

In contrast to the U.S., semiconductors in Europe (and Japan) were developed and exploited by existing large electronics firms. It seems reasonable to suppose that a similar pattern will follow with the development and exploitation of microelectronics. This could mean that while the information technology has generated many new jobs in the U.S., this may not be so true in Europe.

In Europe the widespread adoption of microelectronics might simply accelerate the process of job-replacing rationalization in

---

*In terms of workers created/$ million of turnover, this yields the figures:

Mature corporations	7
Innovative companies	50
Young, high-tech. companies	410

the manufacturing sector (while at the same time increasing the potential for expanding the 'self-service' sector). In other words, because of the high level of entrepreneurial activity in the U.S., particularly in high-technology areas, rationalization will be accompanied by vigorous new product development: in Western Europe, with a greater reliance on traditional sectors in which the primary mode of development is 'incremental', the potential for rationalization is high, but the prospects for new product development are relatively lower.

There is, in fact, also evidence to suggest that, because of different cultural and social factors, the employment 'shake-out' in traditional areas of U.S. industry (shoes, textile, ship-building) occurred during the past few decades, whereas in Europe it has only really begun to add significantly to unemployment.

(ii) Qualitative changes

As well as the quantitative changes outlined above, there appear to have been some recent qualitative changes in the structure of unemployment in the advanced economies. Specifically, there seems to be a growing mis-match between job vacancies and the qualifications and expectations of sections of the unemployed. Because of this, and despite high levels of unemployment, in the Netherlands, for example, in some areas (e.g. construction), companies are forced to import foreign labour. Aubert (1978) has pointed to a similar situation existing in France. Thus the situation of high unemployment co-existing with large numbers of vacancies exists in some countries.

Western educational systems continue to produce large numbers of highly-skilled specialists; the question is, are job opportunities for these specialists expanding at a similar rate? According to several observers, the answer to this question is no, and there is likely to be a growing surplus of the highly educated, with a consequent under-utilization of knowledge and skills. According to Harman (1978), commenting on the situation in the United States:

. . . the proportion of the adult labour force with one or more years of college rose from 19% in 1960 to 27% in 1970. However, the proportion of total employment represented by managerial, administrative, technical and professional positions rose more slowly, going from 20% in 1960 to 22% in 1970 (as contrasted with nearly 50% of young adults who expect these kinds of work). . . . more of the future work force will be better educated and will demand jobs that offer challenge, growth and self-fulfilment; since there will not be enough such jobs to go round, many workers will become disaffected.

The data presented in Table 4.3 show the supply of, and demand for, labour of different educational levels in the Netherlands in 1970, and projections for the next 20 years. It shows

Table 4.3. *Labour Supply and Demand in the Netherlands by levels of Education (%)*

	1970	1980	1990	2000
Lower level				
Supply	48	27	18	12
Demand	48	37	25	20
Medium level				
Supply	46	61	66	69
Demand	47	57	67	70
Higher level				
Supply	6	12	16	19
Demand	5	6	8	10

Source: J. Passenier, Central Planning Office, in the Dutch Official Gazette, 1978.

that while there was only a slight mis-match (surplus) between the supply of, and demand for labour with high educational levels in 1970, this mis-match is likely to grow to very high proportions by the year 2000 (Kanters, 1978).*

---

*It also posits a significant mis-match in supply and demand for workers with low educational levels, this time with a supply deficit.

A pattern which seems to have become apparent in several advanced economies during the past 5 years or so is the employment of graduates in jobs previously taken by non-graduates. For example, more women graduates are being employed in secretarial work and more science and engineering graduates are working as technicians.

So, as well as increasing *levels* of employment in most advanced economies during the 1970s, there are signs that some *qualitative* changes are also occurring. Whereas past developments have resulted in the displacement mainly of unskilled labour and of skilled artisans in some traditional areas, it might be that increasing numbers of the highly educated will in future experience increasing difficulty in finding employment commensurate with their skills. However, while it is possible to link at least part of the job loss among the unskilled and semi-skilled to specific changes in technology and technique, in the case of the highly educated such a connection is not so apparent.

It seems logical to suppose that as industry develops, manufactures, and adopts more and more sophisticated products and technology, the demand for technical graduates will increase. If, however, the growth in supply of graduates outstrips industry's demand for them, then this will result in their unemployment or employment in lower-level jobs. It might be, therefore, that while the increase in overall unemployment in most Western economies is largely structural in nature, unemployment among the highly educated is related more to demand factors.

CHAPTER 5

CASE STUDIES OF THE IMPACT OF TECHNICAL CHANGE ON EMPLOYMENT

As indicated in Chapter 2, there appears to be strong evidence to support a structuralist interpretation of some contemporary problems of manufacturing employment.* This evidence was, however, presented at a highly aggregated level, and it is likely that analysis at the level of specific industry sectors and specific technologies could go some way towards providing a more detailed understanding of the role technical change has played in affecting employment in industry during the post-war era.

Current concern about the potential impact of new technology on employment is not unique. In the 1950s there was considerable concern in the American trade unions in particular about the effects of automation and computerization on levels of employment: the massive unemployment predicted as a result of these radical new technologies did not materialize, partly because of expansionary policies in the U.S. (and the Vietnam War), and partly because of the time it took for them to diffuse throughout U.S. industry. Concern today is based primarily around an equally radical new technology, the microprocessor, and it might be that studying what has happened during the past 30 years will aid in better understanding what is likely to happen in the future.

---

*This must not be taken to suggest that levels of aggregate are unimportant. Aggregate demand is extremely important; however, explanations and prescriptions couched *solely* in terms of aggregate demand provide an insufficient guide.

As mentioned in Chapter 3, a *pattern of jobless growth* has been long established in the agricultural sector, and Figure 3.3 showed that while employment in agriculture in the U.K. declined between 1953 and 1975 by about 50%, agricultural production increased by about 160%. It is extremely difficult to ascribe quantiatively the major increases in yield to specific causes, and undoubtedly a variety of diverse factors have each made their separate — but often interrelated — contribution, e.g. advances in crop breeding and in husbandry; more efficient fertilizers and herbicides; improved farmer education and advisory services; increased mechanization.* There can be little doubt, however, that the major impact on manpower requirement was brought about through mechanization.

Table 5.1 shows the numbers of several classes of powered machines in the U.K. agriculture in 1946 and 1971. It demonstrates a vast increase in agricultural power and the displacement

Table 5.1. *Powered Machines in U.K. Agriculture, 1946 and 1971*

Thousands of:	1946	1971
Combine harvesters	3.5	66.0
Grain driers	1.0	63.5
Motor transport	61.8	130.3

Source: Blaxter (1973).

of a great deal of labour. Nor is the picture quite that simple. Between 1946 and 1971 the average power — and hence the production capability — of each of the various agricultural machines has also risen greatly, which has further reduced farm labour requirements.

---

*Some indication of the relative importance of mechanization was given in the Report of the Canadian Commission on Farm Machinery (1971). This report estimated that the annual benefit from improvements in farm machinery of $2-300 million probably exceeded the benefits from all other agricultural improvements.

It is possible to relate the increase in the use of specific machines to the decline in employment which accompanied their adoption. Figure 5.1 shows the decline in employment of seasonal workers in the U.K. that accompanied the increasing use by farmers of automatic potato harvesters between 1960

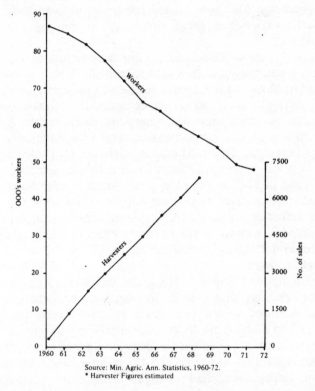

Source: Min. Agric. Ann. Statistics, 1960-72.
* Harvester Figures estimated

Figure 5.1. Seasonal employees in potato harvesting and potato harvester sales (harvester figures estimated), 1960-72.

and 1968. These machines began to enter the U.K. market in small numbers during the late 1950s, and their numbers increased rapidly from 1960 onwards. Before this, seasonal employment in potato harvesting was fairly stable (89,000 in 1957;

63

87,000 in 1959); between 1960 and 1968 seasonal employment fell by 40%, and has subsequently continued to decline. The majority of these seasonal workers are itinerants, who follow the potato crop from Scotland down to southern England over a period of months. Many of them will have been doing this for generations and their displacement by machinery, coupled to their generally low educational level, means that they would inevitably experience great difficulty in finding alternative employment.

Figure 5.2 shows the rapid decline in the number of seasonal workers employed in cotton activities in the U.S. between 1951 and 1970, along with increase in use of automatic cotton harvesters over the same period: once again, the employment displacement effects of new machinery are considerable. By 1970 about 90% of all U.S. cotton was harvested by machinery.

Here, seasonal farmworkers are defined as those who are hired to work on any one farm for less than a continuous 150-day period in the course of a year. In each year most of the workers were engaged in picking cotton; a few were engaged in related activities. Much of the displaced labour — again mostly uneducated — moved to the northern cities in search of alternative employment, and contributed to the problems of social deprivation there.

The manpower required for grain and straw harvesting has also been reduced dramatically through technical change, which has incorporated several previously separated tasks (threshing, binding) into a single machine — the combine harvester. In 1950 the manpower requirement to harvest 25 tons per day was between eight and nine: in 1975 the requirement was two. The machine requirement had changed from three tractors, one threshing machine, one binder and one wagon in 1950 to one combine harvester, one tractor and one wagon in 1975.

Perhaps the greatest impact on farm manpower requirements was brought about through the substitution of tractor-power for horse-power. In the U.S.A. in the 1920s and 1930s one tractor plus one operator replaced two teamsters, six horses and an individual who serviced this team (shoeing, veterinary,

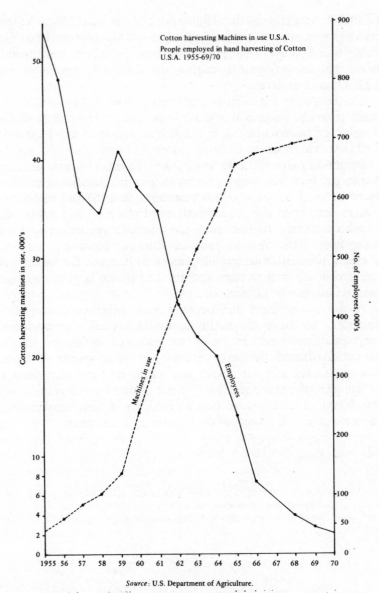

Cotton harvesting Machines in use U.S.A.

People employed in hand harvesting of Cotton U.S.A. 1955-69/70

Cotton harvesting machines in use, 000's

No. of employees, 000's

Machines in use

Employees

Source: U.S. Department of Agriculture.

Figure 5.2 Cotton harvesting machines in use, U.S.A. People employed in hand harvesting of Cotton, U.S.A., 1955–69/70.

65

tackle).* As early as the 1920s Ford alone was selling 50,000 tractors per annum with a consequent displacement of something like 100,000 teamsters each year. The contribution this made to unemployment during the great depression of the 1930s was considerable.

Tractors were not used to any great extent in Western Europe until after the Second World War. Between 1939 and 1960 the number of tractors in use in the U.K. increased from 55,000 to 370,000. The number of horses in use in farming fell during the same period from 550,000 to 46,000.† Taking the ratio of three horses per teamster, this represents a loss in agricultural employment in the U.K. of 170,000 teamsters. In 1965 the number of tractors in use in the nine countries of the EEC was 3,446,000 — which clearly represents a considerable reduction in farm manpower. This loss in jobs in Europe, however, occurred during a time of considerable growth in demand for workers in the secondary and tertiary sectors, and hence largely went unmarked outside of farming circles.

As farm machinery has become more productive and more complex, so have the skill requirements of the operator/ mechanic increased. In order to take full advantage of the potential offered by better machinery, new breeds of crops, new fertilizers and herbicides and improved farm management techniques, the skills required by the farmer have also increased considerably, and a new breed of highly skilled, professional farm managers has emerged during the post-war years.

---

*The specialized skills of this worker were made redundant and there was a parallel growth in demand for mechanical skills.

†Figures for tractors and horses in Europe and the U.S.A. in 1948–52 and 1966 are:

	Europe		U.S.A.	
	1948–52	1966	1948–52	1966
Horses	16.5m	9.1m	7.7m	2.8m
Tractors	1.0m	5.2m	3.6m	4.8m

Summary

(a) During the post-war era, a pattern of jobless growth has become established in the agricultural sector in the advanced economies of the West.

(b) Most of the considerable job loss in agriculture during this period was the result of farm mechanization.

(c) Mechanization makes a number of specialist skills relating to the use of horses largely redundant.

(d) At the same time, a new breed of operator/mechanic has emerged, and the professional skill requirements of the farmer have increased considerably.

5(ii) MECHANIZATION OF THE U.K. COAL MINING INDUSTRY*

Up until the Second World War, diffusion of mechanization within the U.K. coal mining industry was extremely slow. The percentage of total output cut by machine had taken 25 years to increase from 1.4% in 1900 to just under 20%, and a further 13 years to reach 60% in 1938. This was partly due to the availability of cheap and abundant labour in the U.K. and also to the highly fragmented nature of the industry which meant that few of the small colliery companies were willing to invest in the development of radically new equipment. This situation changed following nationalization of the industry in 1947.

In 1947 the Coal Board concentrated on the installation of machinery underground at the face. This did have an effect on productivity, with output per man shift (OMS) increasing from 20.6 cwt in 1946 to 24.5 cwt in 1951. However, the returns from underground mechanization began to fall off in 1952 and OMS stuck at 24 cwt and did not rise again until 1958. In 1950/1 the limits of existing concepts of underground mechanization had been reached, and only new advances in technique could sustain further productivity increases.

*This section is taken largely from the results of a detailed study of the mechanization of coal mining in the U.K. by Townsend (1976).

67

A number of different machines were developed, but in the end it was the Anderton Shearer-leader (ASL), a long-face cutting system, which proved the most robust, versatile and productive machine in the conditions prevailing in most British mines. Figure 5.3 illustrates the ASL's progress up to 1972 by comparison with all mechanization. It also shows the increase in the percentage of total production that was won at mechanized faces.

Parallel with the development and diffusion of the ASL, the coal industry began to experience major competition from other sources of energy. For example fuel oil from British-based refineries had increased in price by only half as much as coal from 1950 to 1960, and technical changes in the capital equipment of the gas, rail and steel industries had made major changes in their fuel consumption, which resulted in a drastic reduction in demand for coal. Thus, with the industry experiencing considerable pressure for contraction of its output, the impetus to mechanize the face to drastically increase efficiency and hence cost competitiveness assumed even greater urgency.

Along with increased mechanization, the Coal Board embarked on a programme of rationalization and began to close large numbers of marginal and unprofitable pits. As a result, the total number of faces declined from 3,603 in 1960 to 997 in 1971, of which 27% were mechanized in 1960 and 89.1% were mechanized in 1971. The OMS increased from 28.9 cwt in 1960/1 to 46 cwt in 1974/5. This increase in productivity was the result both of mechanization and closures of uneconomic pits with consequent concentration on high producing faces. It has been estimated that about 25% of the improvement in OMS from 1963 to 1970 could be attributed to colliery closures.

The rapid diffusion of mechanization produced management problems of using the equipment successfully. Its successful adoption meant that improvements in management and in labour relations were necessary which, generally speaking, were achieved.

Table 5.2 shows manpower and OMS in the U.K. coal industry

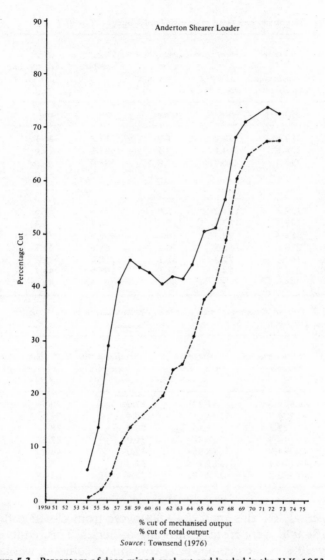

Anderton Shearer Loader

% cut of mechanised output
% cut of total output
Source: Townsend (1976)

Figure 5.3. Percentage of deep mined coal cut and loaded in the U.K. 1953-72

between 1952 and 1970/1. It can be seen that there was a total manpower reduction in the industry of 427,000 (60%) during

Table 5.2. *Manpower and OMS in British Coal Mining, 1952–70/1*

Year	Manpower at continuing collieries	Manpower at collieries now closed	Manpower at new openings	Total manpower	OMS continuing collieries	OMS Index (1961 = 100)
	000s	000s	000s	000s	cwt	
1952	354.6	357.2	1.9	717.3	26.1	
1958	358.5	314.1	8.5	681.1	27.6	
1960	323.4	246.8	12.8	583.0	–	
1961	–	–	–	–	32.0	100
1962	–	–	–	–	34.1	107
1963/4	–	–	–	–	36.0	113
1964/5	299.8	154.7	22.8	477.3	37.3	117
1965/6	287.6	123.1	25.5	436.2	38.4	120
1966/7	281.4	99.4	28.9	409.7	38.7	121
1967/8	270.6	63.5	30.7	364.8	41.1	128
1968/9	260.3	27.2	31.2	318.7	43.5	136
1969/70	249.8	14.4	31.5	295.7	44.7	140
1970/1	245.7	7.6	33.1	286.4	44.8	140

Table 5.3. *Output, Manpower and Degree of Mechanization in the Yorkshire Coalfield, 1957–63.*

Year	Pithead output (000 tons)	Average no. of workers	Overall output per manshift	Mechanized output as percentage of total
1957	48,874.6	137,827	27.2	20.5
1958	49,104.8	136,457	28.4	24.9
1959	48,423.5	132.161	28.9	28.1
1960	46,418.4	121.864	31.0	32.8
1961	45,094.9	116,554	32.0	44.4
1962	48,718.4	115,298	34.3	58.2
1963	50,396.3	112.771	35.9	68.6

Source: Hepworth *et al.* (1969).

this period. Of this total, 349,600 were from closed collieries, and 108,000 were from continuing collieries. This reduction of nearly 30% in the manpower at continuing collieries was largely the result of mechanization. Thus, between 1952 and 1970/1, up to 15% of labour in the U.K. coal mining industry was displaced through technical developments. Without the benefits of new technical changes similar to those gained in the past, the above rates of rundown in manpower would make the present level of output difficult to maintain. In the near future at least, therefore, redundancies are most likely to occur through colliery closures.

Hepworth *et al.* (1969) have studied in detail the effects of technological change on employment in the Yorkshire coalfield between 1957 and 1965. Their data relating to output, manpower and the degree of mechanization in the Yorkshire coalfield between 1957 and 1963 are set out in Table 5.3.

According to the Coal Board (1964) the fall in employment opportunities occasioned by mechanisation would be accommodated through wastage. By wastage the Board meant involuntary wastage and presumably some normal level of voluntary wastage. Involuntary wastage referred to losses of manpower through deaths, disability, retirement, dismissals because of indiscipline, but not redundancy through redundant workers are normally included by the Board in their statistics of involuntary wastage. Voluntary wastage referred to all losses occurring because of workers leaving the industry of their own accord. Although the Board stated that miners would not be made redundant because of mechanisation, it did not guarantee all miners who might be displaced by machinery would enjoy their customary level of earnings. There existed an agreement between the Board and the Union whereby workers are guaranteed 75 percent of their previous earnings for a period of 26 weeks after downgrading.*
The analysis of the employment effects of mechanisation must, therefore, proceed by an examination of changes in the two components of wastage and also available information on downgrading.

Unlike other divisions of the National Coal Board, the Yorkshire Division did not have to make any serious adjustments to the change of the fortunes of the industry after

---

*This would have meant that a pieceworker's earnings could fall to the equivalent of the National Grade 1 day wage rate.

1957 until 1967. The only marked effect was the application of the compulsory retirement rule which resulted in the loss of 2000 miners aged 65 and over between 1959 and 1960. Apart from this 'once and for all change' the various components of involuntary wastage remained fairly constant. Of course in an industry such as mining which is subject to a high level of labour turnover a policy of not replacing workers who had not left on their own accord could lead to a considerable reduction in the size of the labour force. For example, the sum of the annual voluntary wastage figures for the years 1958 to 1963 would more than account for the decline in the labour force over the period 1957 to 1963, assuming there had been no attempt at replacement. Such a policy would not normally be carried out for it would seriously affect the age and occupational structure (and hence efficiency) of the labour force, but it does indicate the possibilities of reducing manpower level that could be accomplished.

Merely to cease recruitment and allow involuntary wastage to reduce the labour force would not, of course, have removed the possibilities of technological unemployment. If the stream of potential recruits to the coal industry could not find jobs in other industries then there would be general unemployment. Alternatively, if these workers were absorbed in other industries then wages in other industries might become depressed relative to those obtaining in coal mining. The general level of unemployment in the coalfield did not alter significantly over the period under observation. It was, however, impossible to tell whether relative wages had altered since there had been extensive changes in the size and geographical coverage of the sample conducted by the Ministry of Labour.

The fact that the general level of unemployment remained constant, the marked rise in voluntary wastage of miners in 1960 and 1961 and in 1964, and instances of downgrading suggested a common pattern whereby *the labour displacement effects of mechanisation did not lead to serious disturbances.*

The rise in voluntary wastage may have reflected the widening of employment opportunities for people in the mining villages - this is the pull effect. At the same time it could also be due to *the decline in promotion prospects that might accompany mechanisation*. This latter possibility could occur if mechanisation meant that haulage workers who were face-trained had to wait longer for vacancies at the coalfaces because there were fewer face jobs and because displaced face workers had to be accommodated first. Of course, technological change might not be uneven in its incidence. If haulage work is also mechanised then there could be a balanced reduction in manpower which could be effected at the point of recruitment. Alternatively if mechanisation increases the rate of face advance then displaced workers could be absorbed in highly-paid development work.

In our surveys at pits we did not come across any haulage workers who felt that their promotion prospects had been adversely affected by mechanisation nor did we meet any face workers who had been downgraded. We did, however, hear of pits where an increase in the numbers of face-trained workers not working at the face was giving rise to concern. For example, at Glass Houghton Colliery there was a strike in April 1964 whose formal cause was that seven face workers had been asked to do haulage jobs for which they would only be paid at the day-wage rate.* A leaflet issued by the strikers stated that mechanisation was resulting in downgrading for workers. The downgrading problem can be important since the guaranteed payment for downgrading operates for only a limited period, and has deeper implications, for within the context of the industry's wage structure the differential between the piece-rate face workers and day-wage

*We say 'formal' cause because it has been alleged that the limiting of the strike owed much to political struggles within the NUM and the failure of the strikers to obtain support from outside their Area was interpreted as a refusal of the Doncaster miners to support the campaign of a potential West Yorkshire candidate for the position of compensation agent. After the strike the Divisional Board did, however, suggest investigating the possibilities of two-shift working as a solution to the problem of downgrading.

haulage workers has been widening as a result of mechanisation. The Glass Houghton strikers attempted to widen the area of support by linking their cause with that of all day-wage workers who had just been offered an eight shillings per week increase by the National Coal Board.

It is difficult, if not impossible, to disentangle the relative importance of the 'pull' and 'push' effects affecting labour mobility in the coalfield. In some areas, such as Barnsley and Doncaster, pits have had great difficulty in attracting and retaining labour and transferees from pits in Scotland and Durham have been useful additions to the local labour supplies. The pits in our sample survey had differeing experiences. One pit opened out new districts and took on more labour whilst another pit lost labour not through an act of deliberate policy but simply because it could not attract sufficient labour locally. Indeed the contrast between the experiences of individual pits and of the coalfield as a whole points to a further stage in the analysis of labour displacement by technological change. The National Coal Board is a multiplant firm and its objective of an output of 150 million tons a year at minimum cost implies that some attempt will be made to allocate 'output quotas' between pits of differing efficiencies. Cost reducing innovations in Yorkshire may, therefore, be a cause of labour displacement in other coalfields. This was the argument of the authors of *A Plan for Miners* who state that, for the coal industry as a whole 'the coincidence of both technical changes (i.e. mechanisation and pit reconstruction schemes) has had profound effects. Both of them were labour saving in character; indeed they account for more of the fall in manpower than does the decline in coal sales'.*

So far the analysis has been directed as analysing the effects of mechanisation on the general level of employment of miners. Technological change, however, usually alters the composition of skills required. There has, in fact, been a rise

*NUM (derbyshire Area), *A Plan for Miners* (Chesterfield, 1964, p. 2, italics in the original).

74

in the demand for electricians and fitters.

Despite the high standards of its craft schemes the Divisional Board has experienced great difficulty in attracting and retaining craftsmen owing to competition from other industries. One colliery manager felt that the Board's training schemes set too high a standard. It was designed to produce chief electricians and fitters for whom there were only a limited number of jobs at pit level. Some training schemes, he felt, ought to be devised to produce 'run-of-the-mine' craftsmen. Such a policy might, of course, reduce wastage by excluding transferable skills from training schemes.

Hepworth *et al.* reached the following conclusions:

1. The technological changes that have occurred in the Yorkshire coalfield have been labour saving, but this effect has been obscured by the fact that planned displacement of labour in the coalfield has on occasions been less than actual labour wastage.
2. There appeared to have been a lack of preparation and training for mechanisation which may have stemmed from weaknesses in the Board's organisation and the pressure to check the fall in the demand for coal. Lack of preparation and training have accounted for the adverse criticisms of mechanisation we received and the rise in the accident rate.
3. Mechanisation did not completely resolve the wages problem. Higher fall back rates have reduced the *tendency* for allowances to form a substantial portion of earnings.
4. Strike activity has fallen, but this cannot be solely attributed to mechanisation. There was a consolidation of price lists on conventional faces giving similar advantages to those obtained on power loaded faces. The higher the rate of productivity on mechanised faces, however, giving more scope for absorbing wage pressures. Intra and inter-shifts can still arise on mechanised faces though they are less pronounced.

Summary

(a) Post-war mechanization in the British coal mining industry has made a major contribution to increased productivity.

(b) Mechanization resulted in the loss of up to 15% of workers between 1952 and 1971.

(c) In the Yorkshire coalfield at least, labour displacement due to technical changes was often less than natural labour wastage. Therefore, its displacement effects were largely obscured.

(d) The successful adoption of automation required improvements in the quality of management and in labour relations.

(e) Lack of adequate preparation and training caused a great deal of adverse criticism of mechanization and a rise in the accident rate.

(f) The use of advanced new machinery imposed the requirements for new skills, notably in electronics.

5(iii) CANADIAN RAILWAYS

Peitchinis (1978) has reported the employment effects of technical change in the Canadian railway system. He concentrated specifically on the substitution of the diesel locomotive, and subsequently the electric locomotive, for the steam locomotive during the 1950s and the 1960s respectively.

The main impacts of dieselization were:

— it facilitated a substantial increase in the number of cars per train. This reduced the number of train units and affected the employment of all occupations constituting a train crew, i.e. engine drivers, conductors and brakemen;

— it provided the ability for trains to operate on longer runs. This caused the closure of a large number of stations, thus affecting the employment of station service personnel, from station masters to cleaners;

— it made redundant the locomotive firemen and affected the employment activities of other workers whose responsibilities

76

related to the maintenance of the steam locomotive and the generation of its motive power.

Table 5.4 lists the changes in manpower employed in fifteen different classes of railway occupations to dieselization and electrification. Only three groups recorded increases in employment. These were the professional, technical and staff assistance groups; the signal and electrical transmission foreman and signal and interlocker maintenance and mechanics group; the work equipment operators, maintenance and mechanics group.

According to Peitchinis, only a relatively small number of railway employees were released from employment because of the new locomotive systems, despite the fact that total employment fell by 51,963 during dieselization (1956–66) and by a further 19,961 during electrification (1966–76). Some of this decrease in employment resulted from falling passenger traffic which had been taking place for some time and which was not related directly to the introduction of the substitute technology.

The main impact of the substitution of the steam locomotive with a different locomotive was a massive *redistribution* of employment within the industry:

Some of the affected employees were relocated to other stations, some were given alternative work functions not requiring retraining, some were relocated and allowed time to acquire new work knowledge on the job, some were allowed to take early retirement, and some elected to leave railway employment. The capital investment involved in the dieselization process was substantial, and its introduction was gradual, over a number of years. The gradualness facilitated the necessary manpower and employment adjustments, and as a result, it was possible to introduce satisfactory accommodative arrangements even in relation to occupations that were rendered redundant, such as that of the locomotive fireman.

Between 1956 and 1976 the volume of freight traffic increased by 40%, while at the same time employment in the industry decreased by the same amount. This increase in efficiency

Table 5.4. *Employment in Canadian Railways (1956, 1966, 1976)*

	1976 No.	1966 No.	1956 No.	% changes		
				1956–66	1966–76	1956–76
1. Managerial and supervisory	6,126	6,189	6,485	−4.6	−1.0	−5.5
2. Professional, technical and staff assistants	7,108	5,196	2,285	+127.4	+36.8	+211.1
3. Chief clerks, assistant chief clerks and office supervisors	1,115	1,623	1,769	−8.3	−31.3	−37.0
4. Clerks and related occupations	14,601	16,972	21,569	−21.3	−14.0	−32.3
5. Bridge and building tradesmen and bridge operators	1,949	2,893	4,055	−28.7	−32.6	−51.9
6. Work equipment operators, maintainers and mechanics	2,488	1,399	1,386	+0.9	+77.8	+79.5
7. Signal and electrical transmission foremen, and signal and interlocker maintainers and mechanics	1,470	1,485	789	+88.2	+1.0	+86.3
8. Blacksmiths and boilermakers	654	724	1,669	−56.6	−9.7	−60.8
9. Carmen	8,297	9,093	11,945	−23.9	−8.8	−30.5
10. Machinists and moulders	3,380	3,396	5,306	−36.0	−0.5	−36.3
11. Station agents, telegraphers, caretaker agents and levermen	2,355	4,577	7,158	−36.1	−48.5	−67.1
12. Freight handlers and freight shed operators	2,945	5,644	5,989	−5.8	+47.8	−50.8
13. Road freight brakemen	5,714	5,104	6,769	−24.6	+12.0	−15.6
14. Engine drivers and motormen	5,296	5,177	6,845	−24.4	+2.3	−22.6
15. Firemen and helpers	681	3,244	7,551	−57.0	−79.0	−91.0
Grand total Railway operations	109,745	129,706	181,659	−28.6	−15.4	−39.6
Freight traffic: in tons	262.9^m	214.4^m	187.6^m	+14.3	+22.6	+40.1

Sources: D.B.S. (Statistics Canada) *Railway Transport* (Catalogue No. S2-212 Employment; 52–205 freight traffic), Annual.

contributed only minimally to employment redistribution within the railway industry. Thus, Peitchinis concludes that:

> . . . it is easier to approximate accurately the nature of manpower that will be required for a different kind of substitute technology, than it is to determine the employment and employment distribution effects of increases in efficiency.

Summary

(a) The main employment effect of the dieselization and subsequent electrification of Canadian railways was one of massive job redistribution rather than widespread redundancy.
(b) The adoption of the new technology was gradual, which greatly facilitated the occupational readjustment process.
(c) Much of the job loss in the industry over the period 1956–76 was related to demand factors, i.e. the long-established fall in the volume of passenger traffic.

5(iv) THE TEXTILE MACHINERY INDUSTRY

Since 1945 textile machinery has undergone a technological revolution. Not only has the *pace* of technical change greatly increased, but its *nature* has changed dramatically as well, in that much of the change has become technically more radical in nature and has increasingly embodied techniques from other areas, e.g. aerodynamics, electronics, chemical technology. This has had both a qualitative and a quantitative impact on employment in the textile machinery industry. In the first place, it has required changes in the *type* of manpower employed in the industry: in the second place it has affected the *level* of employment as the result of a change in international competitiveness, which has become increasingly based on the technical sophistication of textile machinery (Rothwell, 1977).

A recent detailed study of post-war innovation in textile

machinery in Western Europe has clearly shown that, in general, it is those companies which have been 'technically progressive' that have survived and prospered during the post-Second World War years (Rothwell, 1976). A number of companies have, in contrast, suffered drastic decline during this period from positions of eminence to positions of near oblivion today primarily because they failed sufficiently to update existing models and to produce new generations of machinery. There exists also very strong evidence to suggest that the technical sophistication of textile machinery plays a dominant role in determining its export competitiveness.

The position of the U.K. industry has been one of decline, and this decline has been the result primarily of the failure of many U.K. textile machinery firms to undertake vigorous programmes of technical development (Rothwell, 1977(a)). As a result, the U.K.'s share of world trade in textile machinery declined from 30% in 1954 to 11% in 1975. At the same time, employment in the industry dropped from 75,000 in 1951 to 35,000 in 1973. This fall in level of employment was the result mainly of loss of market share due to a decline in 'technical change' international competitiveness, rather than the rationalization of manufacturing processes.

The above, while illustrating the importance to commercial success (and hence employment) of technical change *per se*, fails to indicate the relative importance of the different types of technical change, i.e. large-step, 'radical' change or small-step, 'incremental' change. With respect to this question, there is no doubt that a number of instances can be quoted where the introduction of a radical innovation has led to the rapid growth of new firms or new divisions within a firm. Probably the most famous examples of this are the establishment of the enormously successful Sulzer Weaving Section in Sulzer Brothers following the introduction of the revolutionary Sulzer Flying Gripper Weaving Machine, and the rapid growth of the Kovoslav National Corporation in Czechoslovakia following its commercial introduction of the new open-end spinning technique. In most areas, in fact, while short-term prosperity could be insured through simple 'product improvement' innovation, in the longer term more radical innovation has been necessary to maintain the firm's competitive position and foster growth (Rothwell, 1977).

The question is, what are the manpower implications of this? Are there significant manpower-related differences in the factors associated with the generation of successful radical innovations and those associated with the production of successful incremental innovations?

Table 5.5 shows the (averaged) characteristics of the development departments in twenty Western European companies which were *successful* in producing radical textile machinery innovations (radical innovators) and in fifteen companies which produced only small-step innovations (incremental innovators). (It must be noted at the outset that radical innovators had on average three times the employment of incremental innovators.)

The data presented in Table 5.5 suggest that *successful* radical innovations are associated with a formal R & D Department staffed by graduate-level engineers and/or scientists (particularly the former). Incremental innovations, in contrast, tend to occur in a D & D Department staffed primarily by non-graduate engineers. The R & D Department will, of course, be capable of producing incremental as well as radical innovations: the point is, without expert external assistance, the D & D Department will generally be unable to cope with radical technical change. Moreover, an analysis of eight *unsuccessful* radical innovations showed that in seven cases, lack of in-house technical expertise (resulting in the inability to solve technical problems) made a major contribution to failure. Further, several companies quoted a lack of skilled technical manpower as posing the major barrier to their endeavours to innovate.

The employment of technically skilled managers, particularly graduate-level managers, is also increasingly important to the successful outcome of radical textile machinery innovations. Out of a sample of twenty successful radical innovators and fifteen successful incremental innovators, 55% of chief executives were qualified to chartered engineer level (35% graduates)

81

Table 5.5. *Characteristics in the development department — radical and incremental innovators*

Question	Response	Classification			
		Radical		Incremental	
			Conc.		Conc.
Does the firm have a formal R & D Department?	Yes No	14 6		2 13	
If not, does the firm have a formal D & D department?	Yes No	5 1		1 2	
Does the firm have: a. Both b. Neither		6 1		1 2	
How many non-graduate engineers were associated with development work at the time of the project (average no./firm)?		6	0.8%	3	1.3%
How many graduate engineers were associated with development work at the time of the project (average no./firm possessing graduates)?		3.4[a]	0.45%	1.7[a]	0.75%
How many graduate scientists were associated with development work at the time of the project (average no./firm possessing graduate scientists)?		2.2[b]	0.3%	2.0[b]	0.88%

a. These are the average number for firms that actually employed graduate engineers. *Two radical innovators and seven incremental innovators did not employ a single graduate engineer in development.*

b. These are the average number for firms that actually employed graduate scientists. *Seven radical and thirteen incremental innovators did not employ a single graduate scientist in development.*

whereas in the case of incremental innovators only 35% were qualified to this level (20% graduates).

Thus, the increasingly radical nature of technical change in the textile machinery area during the post-war years has meant an increasing requirement for companies to employ highly-skilled technical specialists. This is true not only for the development department, but also for those involved in technical service activities. Failure to employ such specialists results in a lack of international competitiveness with a consequent fall in sector employment.*

Summary

As the nature of technical change has become increasingly radical in the textile machinery area, this has had two major manpower implications:
(a) It has greatly increased the need for highly-skilled technical specialists in management, R & D and Servicing.
(b) It has intensified international technical change competition. Lack of technical change competitiveness has resulted in the loss of a great number of jobs in the U.K.

5(v) THE TEXTILE INDUSTRY

Section iv has described the rate and nature of technical change in textile machinery during the post-war years. In this section the impact of this technical change on manpower requirements

---

*While the U.K. textile machinery industry's share of world trade has declined since the early 1950s, the share taken by West Germany increased from about 18% in 1954 to about 35% in 1973. The proposition that differences in technical manpower levels offer an explanation for the superior performance of the West German textile machinery industry over its U.K. counterpart is an attractive one, as the following figures suggest:

West Germany Percentage of total employees which are 'technical employees' in 1974 — 16.4%. 10% of employees are occupied in 'R & D and Construction'.

U.K. Concentration of scientific, technical and draughting personnel in 1973 — 5.6%.

in the textile industry — and in particular on the staple fibre spinning process — are detailed.

(i) Aggregate view

The principal development trends in textile machinery during the post-Second World War years have been geared towards three prime ends: (1) increasing the productivity of individual units, (2) reducing the number of operations required in a particular process, and (3) increasing the amount of automatic transfer between operations. Points (2) and (3) in particular have had the prime objective of reducing manpower requirements in the mill. This has been especially important in the developed countries where, for many years, there existed a shortage of skilled operatives, and where relatively high wage levels rendered labour-intensive processes uncompetitive in the face of increasing textile production from expanding textile industries in the low labour cost developing countries. As a consequence of this the textile industries in the advanced economies have changed from labour-intensive, craft industries, to the capital-intensive, machine-orientated industries of today. This is demonstrated in Table 5.6 for the weaving process in the U.K.

Table 5.6. *Percentage of Value Added in Weaving*

	Labour cost	Capital cost	Power, building, profit, etc.
1955	60	20	20
1970	25	70	5

Increases in labour productivity in the U.K. spinning and weaving industries between 1950 and 1970 are shown in Table 5.7. A high proportion of these increases in labour productivity can be ascribed to the increased use of new and improved textile processing machinery.

Changes in the relationship between human effort and textile production as a result of technical change are graphically

84

Table 5.7. *Output, Employment and Productivity in the U.K. Spinning and Weaving Industries (Cotton and Man-Made Fibres)*

	1950	1960	1970
Spinning			
Output (m. lb)	943	640	441
Employment ('000)	107	63.7	32.6
Productivity (m. lb/'000)	8.8	10.04	13.53
Weaving			
Output (m. Linear yd)	2,830	1,911	1,216
Employment ('000)	129.2	91.3	43.0
Productivity (m. yd)	21.9	23.5	28.3

(Data abstracted from *Quarterly Statistical Review*, Textile Statistics Bureau, Manchester.)

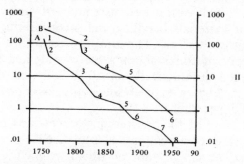

I working hours per 1 kp yarn
II working hours per 100 m fabric

A Spinning	B Weaving
1 Pedal wheel	1 Hand loom, outwork
2 Hargreave	2 Fast shuttle
3 Mule Jenny	3 Mechanical loom
4 Semi mule	4 Multi-loom mill
5 Water driven mule	5 Northrop automatic loom
6 Ring spinning	6 Modern weaving machine
7 RSM	
8 Modern RSM	

Source: *Interface*, Vol. 6, No. 3, 1974 'Innovation and Textiles', David Paton.

Figure 5.4. The change of human effort in the course of time.

illustrated in Fig. 5.4. This shows the change in human effort involved in producing the same quantity of yarn and of cloth during the past 100 years or so. Clearly, technological change has had a significant impact on the labour content of both yarn and fabric production during this period.

The remainder of this paper will concern itself with describing the detailed relationship between technological change and changing manpower requirement in the staple yarn spinning sequence.

(ii) The spinning process

In the early 1930s the first stage of preparation of short fibres for spinning normally employed a single process opening line. This was a highly-automated assembly of units involving a minimum of materials handling and incorporating simple and reliable control devices. The output from this stage was a uniform fleece of fibres about a metre wide and a centimetre thick delivered automatically in 40 lb rolls called 'laps'. The production rate of a typical single process opening line was about 1000 lb per hour.

The next stage of the pre-spinning process was at a much less satisfactory stage of development. It involved:

(i) Carding the lap, 1 yard of which weighed about 1 lb, to produce a 'sliver', of which about 100 yards weighed 1 lb. The production rate of one carding engine (card) was about 8 lb per hour and the sliver was delivered coiled into cylindrical canisters each holding about 10 lb of sliver.

(ii) Drawing the sliver through a succession of accelerating rollers with the object of parallelizing the fibres preparatory to conversion into roving. Typically six slivers from six cans were fed into each drawing unit. The draw ratio would be about six so that the delivered sliver had roughly the same weight per unit length as the individual input slivers and differed only in the degree of orientation of its component fibres. The production rate of each drawing unit was about 100 lb of sliver per hour, delivered in cylindrical cans exactly like those used at the card. To achieve the requisite degree of fibre orientation it was usual to pass all slivers through three successive stages of drawing.

(iii) Production of roving from sliver. This was done on 'spindle and flyer' frames fed from 10 lb cans of sliver and producing roving on bobbins weighing from 1 to 3 lb depending on the fineness of the yarn to be produced by the spinning frames. A typical roving frame would have from 100 to 150 spindles.

A visitor to an early 1950s mill would have been immediately struck by the early-industrial-revolution atmosphere of this stage of yarn manufacture. In the smallest mill equipped with only one opening line (1000 lb/hour) he would have seen 125 cards -- each a large machine occupying about 100 square feet of floor space -- with a part exhausted 40 lb lap of cotton on its feed table and a part-filled 10 lb sliver can under the delivery coiler. Downstream from the cards would be three sequences of drawing each consisting of twelve to fourteen drawing units, each fed from six sliver cans and delivering into a seventh. Downstream again from the draw frame would be the spindle and flyer frames with a total of 250 to 500 spindles each fed from one of the sliver cans delivered by the final draw frames. The input and output of these processes are shown in Table 5.8 along with the corresponding OHP* figures.

Perhaps the dominant feature of the scene was the amount of feeding of material into (creeling) and removal of material from (doffing), the machinery that was being done manually, and the number of cans of sliver about the place. In addition to buffer stocks of full and empty cans there were seven hundred and twenty-five cans actually in use each, at any one time, holding on average 5 lb sliver and each representing a creeling or doffing point requiring more or less frequent manual attendance. At the cards it was necessary to creel in 25 laps per hour and doff 100 cans per hour. The drawframe section presented the

---

*Operative hours per unit of production.

Table 5.8. *Input and Output of Successive Processes and OHP*

Operation and machinery requirement		In	Out	OHP
Carding	— 125 carding engines	125 × 40 lb laps	125 × 10 lb sliver cans	0.703
First drawing	— 12 drawing units	72 × 10 lb sliver cans	12 × 10 lb sliver cans	
Second drawing	— 12 drawing units	72 × 10 lb sliver cans	12 × 10 lb sliver cans	0.547
Third drawing	— 12 drawing units	72 × 10 lb sliver cans	12 × 10 lb sliver cans	
Roving — 350 spindle and flyer units		350 × 10 lb sliver cans	350 × 2 lb sliver cans	1.288
Cardroom general		—	—	0.273
				3.16

scene of most frenzied activity with a need for creeling in 300 cans per hour and doffing a similar number, each creel can remaining in position for about 42 minutes and each of the 36 delivery stations requiring the doffing of a can approximately every 7 minutes. The spindle and flyer frame section was relatively quiet with 350 cans, each remaining in place for about 3½ hours.

It is difficult to give a clear yet concise picture of the tasks involved in marshalling, doffing and creeling sliver cans. The cans themselves were generally 9 or 10 inches in diameter and about 30 inches high — not by any means ideal for handling but necessarily of that shape for proper functioning of the coiling mechanism and the stacking requirements for a satisfactory creel. Doffing required only the removal of the full can followed by deft replacement by an empty can and severance of the sliver. Creeling required timely removal of the emptying can, replacement by a full can and neat and skilful splicing of the new sliver to the tail of the old one.

The above presents a picture of a situation in which there was clearly much scope for the introduction of technological change to reduce the amount of manual handling of material, as well as to increase the productivity of individual production units.

(iii) Technological changes in spinning 1950–68

The main technological changes which have taken place in the pre-spinning and spinning processes are numerous.

The changes which had the most marked impact on the pre-spinning sequence described above are, briefly: (1) increase in card production rates by a factor of about 10, with direct feed from card to draw frame; (2) increase in drawing speeds of the same order as the increase in carding rate. With the old card and draw frame speeds, a 10 lb package was near the optimum: following the ten fold increase in speed, cans of 80 lb to 120 lb are now being used; (3) Improvements in drafting performance (precision of the drafting process) reduced sliver variability to such an extent that it enabled the number of drawing sequences to be reduced from three to two.

The machinery line-up in a modern (1968) mill is shown in Table 5.9. The use of smaller cans for sliver for the delivery from the second stage of drawing is dictated by economic considerations in the design of the fly frame creel.

Table 5.9. *Modern machinery line-up and OHP*

Operation and machinery requirement	In	Out	OHP
Carding — 14 carding engines	Direct feed	14 × 100 lb sliver cans	0.07
First drawing — 4 drawing units	32 × 100 lb sliver cans	4 × 100 lb sliver cans ⎫	
Second drawing — 4 drawing units	32 × 100 lb sliver cans	4 × 40 lb sliver cans ⎬	0.15
Roving — 250 spindle and flyer units	250 × 40 lb cans	250 × 31 lb sliver cans	0.46
Cardroom general	—	—	0.31
			1.01

It is immediately obvious from Table 5.9 that the amount of package handling has been drastically reduced. No creeling is now needed at the cards and the doffing requirement has been reduced from 100 cans per hour to 10. The draw frame creeling requirement has been reduced from 300 cans per hour to 20, and draw frame doffing reduced from 300 cans per hour to 25. This, coupled to the increases in production rate of the individual units, reduced the OHP from a total of 3.16 in 1950 to 1.014 in 1968.

The impact of this technological change on manpower requirements can be summarized as follows: the total number of direct operatives was reduced from 78 in 1950 to 29 in 1968 for 20s cotton, and from 99 in 1950 to 35 in 1968 for 30s cotton: the corresponding figures for indirect labour are 22 and 16½ respectively (20s cotton) and 25 and 19½ respectively (30s cotton).

Clearly between 1950 and 1968 technological change had a major impact on labour requirement in the conventional cotton spinning mill. It is interesting to note that the nature of the technological changes which contributed to this situation were exclusively incremental ('small step' innovations) in nature.

(iv) Post-1968

While contributions to increases in the productivity of the pre-spinning sequence and to a reduction in the manpower component of this aspect of textile production were brought about through incremental technical change, the greatest change in the spinning process itself was the result of a radical innovation, i.e. the introduction of open-end spinning.

Table 5.10 compares the economics of short-staple yarn production for a 1945 spinning mill, a 1963 spinning mill and a modern open-end spinning mill. It demonstrates the move towards greater machine utilization — from one-shift working in 1945 to four-shift working in 1973 — which accompanied the introduction of more modern machinery and which made a significant contribution towards the better economics of yarn production. The table also shows that unit labour costs were reduced by one-half between 1945 and 1963, and by one-half again between 1963 and 1972. These improvements could not have been achieved simply through the use of automated

90

Table 5.10. *Comparison between a Modern Open-end spinning Mill, a Mill Built and installed in 1963, and One Built and installed in 1945**

		1945 mill	*1963 mill*	*1973 mill*
(a)	*Production*			
	Shifts operated	1	3	4
	Hours per week	42.5	112.5	168
	Production per hour (kg)	615	232	156
	Production per week (kg)	26,122	26,122	26,122
	Area (m*)	7,500	3,250	2,100
(b)	*Numbers and types of machinery required*			
	Blowroom	6 scutchers	2 scutchers	1 chute-feed line
	Cards	112	16	5
	Drawframes (deliveries)	240	8	5
	Speedframes (spindles)	2,520	384	—
	Spinning frames (spindles/rotors)	36,000	9,504	1,700
(c)	*Investment*			
	Machinery (S)			871,500
	Ancillary equipment (S)			390,200
	Building (S)			497,000
	Total investment (S)		1,316,000	1,658,700
	Investment per spindle/rotor (S)		(139)	976
	Investment per employee (S)		(18,300)	51,834
(d)	*Labour*			
	Total employees	176	72	32
	Total production workers	168	64	24
	H.O.K.	27.4	9.2	3.9
	Direct workers per 1000 spindles rotors per shift	3.4	1.72	3.5
	Labour cost per week (excluding administration) (S)	16,620†	7200† (2400)	3,024
	Labour cost per 100 kg (S)	63.63†	27.57† (9.19)	11.58

*Plant to produce 1,280,000 kg per annum of 34s-Nm (29 + tex) yarn.

†These figures have been brought up to date to take account of present wage levels. The 1963 figures at 1963 rates are quoted in parentheses.

Source: F. A. Greenwood, 'The Textile Mill of the Future', Proceedings, Textile Institute Conference, Asia and World Textiles. The Textile Institute, 1973.

processes,* or by improved materials handling since, while these would have reduced the work force, they would also have increased machinery costs while the number of machines would have reamined constant. *The real advances were made in the production rate of machines* and, as limits were being approached in ring spinning, open-end spinning was developed which offered a three-fold improvement in productivity per rotor.

Radical technical change has also had a marked impact on the manpower requirement in long-staple (worsted) spinning. Comparison between a best-practice modern conventional worsted spinning mill, and a mill using the radical new REPCO self-twist system, is made below in Table 5.11. This shows that, using the REPCO system, the operative hours per unit of output (OHP) are reduced by almost a third from 3.68 with the conventional sequence to 2.67 with REPCO.

(v) Other factors

(i) *Rationalization and concentration*

Technical change is not, of course, the only factor which has had an impact on labour productivity and manning levels in the textile industry. Greatly increased concentration since 1945, with the formation through rationalization, of large integrated, capital-intensive production units has led to the more efficient use of labour with a consequent reduction in employment.

An interesting example of this is the case of Carrington Viyellas's reorganization of Combined English Mills, which illustrates the complex interaction between the use of up-to-date machinery, product mix, market diversity, management style and employment. Combined English Mills (CEM) had taken full

---

*In the 1950s and early 1960s strenuous efforts were made world wide to develop an automated spinning mill; all these attempts to automate the card room sequence failed in that they did not become established as *commercially* viable systems (although some were successful *technically*).

Table 5.11. *Comparison of a conventional worsted spinning sequence with a REPCO Self-Twist Sequence*

	Machine productivity m/min.	No. of machines deliveries per operative	O.H.P.	Kg. P.O.H.
Conventional short-staple ring spinning — 24s cotton count				
Carding	77 lb/hr/m/c	33 machs	0.039	1155
Drawing	244 m/min.	6 "	0.130	350
Roving	28 "	437 spdls	0.190	239
Spinning	15.6 "	3327 "	0.616 spinners	74
		7092 "	0.289 doffers	157
Winding	914 "	28 "	1.544	29
Conventional long-staple ring spinning — 2/23s worsted count (2/26s Nm)				
Drawing	115.2 m/min	4 spdls	0.300	152
Roving	53.2 "	76 "	0.338	135
Spinning	16.5 "	1082 "	1.177	39
Winding	900 "	29 "	0.915	50
Assembly winding	700 "	35 "	0.447	102
Twisting	41.8 "	519 "	0.505	90
Repco STT — 11.5 worsted count weaving yarn (297 m/min. REPCO) (STT 13 Nm)				
Drawing	115.2 "	4 machs	0.300	152
Roving	53.2 "	76 "	0.338	135
Spinning	297	15.5 machs	0.648 direct	70
			0.118 indirect	385
Twisting	45 "	485 spdls	0.496	92
Winding	1000 "	16 "	0.769	59

Source: Platt Saco Lowell, Helmshore, England. Technical Economy Dept.

advantage of the U.K. government's re-equipment scheme and, when it was acquired by Viyella in 1964, it would have proved difficult to find a mill which had re-equipped to a greater extent than CEM's mill at Leigh. CEM did, however, suffer from the following faults:

  (i) Excess capacity.
 (ii) Lack of positive marketing approach.
(iii) Lack of financial stability.
 (iv) Highly diversified markets.
  (v) Low production efficiencies.
 (vi) High stocks.

As the result of an investigation by Viyella, the following policy of rationalization was adopted:

(a) Reappraise the market situation and CEM's special place therein.

(b) Rationalize the range of products and customers. Give the large customer, who gave consistent and loyal support, reciprocal support.

(c) Cater for Federation customers and gain the consequent savings which stem from the elimination of selling overheads, etc. Aim for vertical integration with its manifold benefits wherever appropriate.

(d) Reappraise the re-equipment programmes, so that new machinery would more effectively improve quality and service to customers. Extend facilities for spinning synthetics.

(e) Close down and liquidate unprofitable plants and excess capacity. Maintain multi-shift working on efficient equipment.

(f) Simplify the management structure. Cut down on the excessive headquarters staff. Ensure closer management links with the Viyella management committee and so have the benefit of its expert services and resources.

(g) Maintain a closer link with other yarn spinning and processing units of the Federation, so that integration would continually take place on all fronts.

(h) Carry out management education, so that they would rediscover its commercial purpose and business acumen.

That this policy, when implemented, proved successful can be judged from Table 5.12.

Thus, this rationalization of the overall operation had a marked impact both on total employment and on labour productivity, which clearly demonstrates *that the more efficient use of existing plant can, in some instances, have as great an effect on employment as the adoption of new technology.*

Table 5.12. *CEM: Before and After*

	Before (1964)	After (1966)
Number of spinning mills	14	7
Number of operating subsidiaries	8	–
Weight produced per year (M. lb)	28	25
Spindles installed	404,000	221,000
Production per spindle year (lb)	69.91	113.0
Average running hours per week per spindle	56.9	110.5
Capital employed (£M)	8.0	3.5
Number employed	3,983	2,318
Production per employee per year (lb)	7,020	9,920
Stocks of yarn	£754,000	£196,000
Productive floor area (M. sq. ft)	4.3	2.0
Management accounting staff	3	7
Centralized staff	43	17
Customers	735	120
Bank balance	−£988,000	+£200,000

(ii) *Changing skills*

Concomitant with changes in the nature of the technology used in the modern textile mill has been a broadening in the range of skills it is necessary for the mill's maintenance personnel to encompass. Perhaps the most notable example of this is the need to employ electronic engineers — or mechanical engineers with some training in electronics — to maintain the ever increasing number of electronic monitoring and control devices incorporated in modern textile machinery.*

---

*In many instances the onus has been on the machinery producer companies to train mill operatives and overlockers in the right usage of their new machines.

A second manpower-related factor deriving from the increased use of electronic devices, which go some way towards reducing the possibilities for manual error and which make it easier to control (greater numbers of) textile machines, is that the skill content of the operative's job has, in many instances, been drastically reduced; this has reduced the need for lengthy apprenticeships in some areas. The majority of workers in the textile industries in a number of European countries today are immigrant labour from less developed countries.

Summary

(a) Developments in textile machinery have greatly increased machine productivity and reduced manpower requirements in the textile industry. The introduction of radical new techniques has accelerated this process.
(b) As a result, the textile industries in the advanced economies have shifted from labour-intensive, craft industries to capital-intensive industries.
(c) Advances in machine technology — and performance — particularly the inclusion of automatic stop-motions and fault indication devices — have led to a high level of de-skilling in the textile industry.
(d) The incorporation of sophisticated electronic devices in a number of areas has created the need for new skills amongst maintenance personnel, especially a knowledge of electronic circuitry.
(e) Vertical integration and rationalization of existing plant has resulted in some job loss.

Although not covered in the text, the following two points are relevant:

(f) In the garment area, a large number of jobs have been lost in Western Europe through an inability to compete with low wage cost developing countries. Some recent, and radical, developments in garment machinery — if adopted — might help to redress this trade imbalance.

(g) The use of computer-aided pattern design and computer pattern control have led to the subcontracting of some aspects of machine maintenance and to the use of software specialists from outside the firm.

5(vi) THE CEMENT INDUSTRY

Cohen-Hadria (1978) has reported the impact of automation on work integration in the cement industry. In the *traditional* cement factory there are three basic stages in the transformation of the raw materials — limestone and clay — into cement. This is represented schematically below:

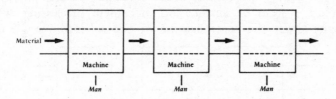

With this system there is a close and direct relationship between man and machine, and the task of each operator is technically defined by the machine he operates (driver of crushing machine, burner, etc.) within each of the functionally separate workshops. It is the operator who receives directly information about the state of material entering and leaving the machine and about the working of the machine itself; it is he who interprets this information and who responds by acting directly on the machine and the materials. Such a job demands a 'complete professional competence'.

Since the 1950s technical developments have meant that electronic and electromechanical controls and sensors have increasingly interposed themselves between each machine and its operator, and these fairly simple controls have meant that certain of the less complex jobs previously done by the operator could be dropped. This new situation is represented in the diagram below:

97

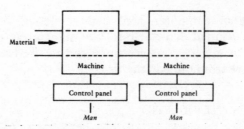

While the man-machine doublet has been replaced by a man-control panel-machine triplet, the separation of tasks as differentiated by the technical process of materials transformation remained.

Towards the end of the 1960s, developments in metrology, data processing and remote control techniques led to a more complete system of automation in cement processing, which brought about the centralization of control into a single unit.

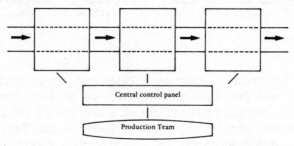

Thus, automation presented a challenge to the traditional division of labour which was based on the different stages of the transformation process as shown above. In parallel to the integration of the production system, there evolved an integration in the job system. Cohen-Hadria differentiates between two kinds of integration, *vertical* — the consolidation of the different levels of job hierarchy — and *horizontal* — the interpenetration of different functions within the cement industry.

Vertical integration

In the non-automated cement factory the functions of the various members of the job hierarchy — production engineer, production manager, production foreman, production workers — were clearly differentiated, and the production workers were localized in their different workshops (each workshop corresponding to one of the three major phases of the materials transformation process). It was only the head of each shift, going from one workshop to the next, who had a global vision of the process at any one time.

With automation, all the information necessary for both the running and the optimization of the complete unit is found concentrated in the central control room. This results in a broad overlapping of the tasks of the different levels of the hierarchy. This vertical consolidation is determined both by the centralization of data, and by a certain levelling-out of skills. While engineers and foremen, for example, differ hugely in their background and training, the type of knowledge necessary to both of them for the optimum running of the process is certainly now closer than was the knowledge each separately required when performing their previously highly differentiated tasks of 'engineer' and 'head of shift'. Thus, traditional levels of job hierarchy are becoming increasingly blurred, and some cement factories are in fact actively reducing the number of these levels.

The relationship between foreman and worker has also altered. In the old system, the foreman was the only polyvalent, with an overall view of the process. With centralized control, it is the operator who acquires this global vision of the process. In order to maintain the traditional division between foreman and workers, some firms have given the position in the control room to the shift foreman, and that of roundsman to the workers. At least one firm has taken the more radical step of having no shift foreman at all, thus defining the role of leader of the team as that played by the operator who happens to be in charge of the control room.

Automation has also resulted in changes in the maintenance department. In the 1950s the foreman of mechanical mainten-

99

ance was the only polyvalent in the maintenance section, and it was his job to integrate the tasks of the variety of craftsmen and unskilled workers then to be found within maintenance.

With the increase in subcontracting that accompanied automation, however, specialization has disappeared within maintenance and has been replaced by polyvalency. The foreman can now no longer be justified solely on the grounds of his technical skills, but more by his capacity for running his team efficiently.

Horizontal integration

In the non-automated cement factory, the division of labour was grounded on the principle of *analytical* division of labour. Thus, within the production unit, each operator had a specific skill corresponding to a given stage in the materials transformation process. The same principle was also the basis of the organization of labour between the different departments, i.e. production, maintenance, quarry, warehouse, etc. Hence, the separation between maintenance and production distinguished those working on the raw material from those working on the machines.

In the automated cement factory this separation of tasks is challenged. It is no longer possible to break the process down into different sub-divisions within the production shift. Each member of the production team must now have a global view of the process, and it becomes a matter of dividing the tasks within a team without any specific *technical demand* defining the *type* of task sharing to be adopted. In some factories, in fact, it is left up to the team to organize themselves as they see fit.

To the extent that other tasks lose their specific nature, the responsibilities of the production team have grown. For example, since technological developments have simplified electrical maintenance — and there is now no longer any need for a professional electrician specialized in electrodynamic relays — simple, almost standardized, repairs are now consigned to the production operators who are familiar with the installations.

Technical developments, and the *growth in subcontracting* that accompanied automation, have rendered redundant certain

100

crafts traditionally found in the cement industry (fitters, iron-smiths, masons, carpenters, etc.). A policy of polyvalence has been adopted to break down the divisions between the different crafts in order to accommodate the disappearance of the need for certain craft (as well as unskilled) workers.

When two tasks have been joined to create a new poly-valent function, this has only occurred following the prior deterioration of each of the two tasks. It is not two crafts which are linked, but a new job created from two unspecified tasks: two 'diminished' skills are joined to create a new 'professional'. Thus, for example, production and maintenance are brought closer together; production as a result of technical change, maintenance essentially through a policy of subcontracting.

Cohen-Hadria proposed a model to describe the evolution of the organization of automated cement factories:

— A qualitative and quantitative reduction of functions filled by the factory in favour of external enterprises.

· either by technical change, some of the functions being pro-grammed into the machines, notably by engineering depart-ments or societies.

· or by a policy of subcontracting aimed at the over- or under-specialized tasks.

— The introduction of functions maintained in the production unit: the formation of a homogenous core (polyvalency, post-rotation) given a certain autonomy (consolidation of the hierarchic ladder) and calling upon different peripheral entities.

Finally, Cohen-Hadria summed up as follows:

— With automation there is not a decrease in the division of labour, but rather a change in the forms it takes: the tech-nical division of tasks within the unit, generally opening the way for an authoritarian and hierarchical type of co-ordination, gives way to a more 'societal' division of labour between all the complementary production units within the same process.

— In the same way it seems easier to see in automation the

transformation of a process of disqualification/over-qualification, rather than simply a stage in this process: one might say, by enlarging this concept, that there is a disqualification of the production unit as a whole, it becoming more and more dependent on designers and manufacturers of automated systems as well as various sub-contractors. On the contrary, within the production unit, the change in the horizontal and vertical distribution of tasks can enable new qualified posts to appear.

Thus, polyvalency in maintenance does imply the disqualification of some professionals, but also the overqualification of a larger number of slightly specialized workers. As for running the plant, the various solutions found aim at giving the workers the most global vision of the process, so that it becomes possible to foresee a new profession in the cement industry, a man who would be both production and maintenance oriented, electrician and a specialist in the process techniques.

— An important question is then that of the professional future of the operator concerned: in the cement industry, agreements allow for the professional advancement of the production and maintenance operators. But one might think that the operators may wish also for an increase in the responsibilities they are allowed to assume, advancement which is seriously menaced by the horizontal and vertical consolidation that we have indicated.

— It is obvious that the evolution we have described makes very difficult any *quantitative* statement about employment: in the petro-chemical industry, according to Coriat (1978), three quarters of the workers responsible for the working of the process are not on the staff of the petrol companies. The lack of precision of this figure from one company to another makes it difficult to evaluate the productivity of automated installations: thus certain Japanese cement factories claim a colossal annual tonnage per worker, which may be only the effect of a policy of massive subcontracting. This may explain the absence of truly convincing global studies of automation and the level of employment or the economic aspects of automation.

— Finally, we shall not dwell on the fact that by subcontracting, large numbers of workers are excluded from the collective wage agreements of the branch to whose functioning they contribute.

Summary

(a) Automation has resulted in the increased centralization of control of cement manufacture.

(b) Automation has resulted in some vertical integration of job functions, with a levelling-out of skills.

(c) Automation has resulted in some horizontal integration of job functions.

(d) A number of specific skills, particularly in maintenance, and several crafts have been rendered redundant by automation.

(e) At a same time new 'polyvalent' tasks are being created.

(f) Automation in the cement industry has led to a dramatic increase in the amount of subcontracting.

5(vii) THE STEEL INDUSTRY

Jacobson (1978) has studied the relationship between technological change and employment in the U.S. steel industry. Although no figures are available linking job loss directly to technical change, there seems no doubt that it has been an important factor in job loss. Figure 5.5 shows the total output in the U.S. steel industry and total output less open-hearth production. The difference reflects the output of basic oxygen furnaces and electric furnaces which represent new technology. From these data it is clear that the U.S. steel industry has undergone a rapid and reasonably complete modernization. Since 1964, output has remained fairly stable.

Figure 5.6 shows employment in the U.S. steel industry

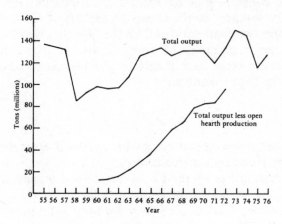

Figure 5.5. Output of the steel industry (1955–76)

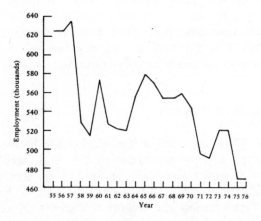

Figure 5.6. Employment in the steel industry (1955–76)

between 1965 and 1976. The sharp drop in employment in 1959 was caused by a 116-day steel strike. Following a large increase around 1964, employment fell at a fairly constant rate during the remainder of the 1960s.

According to Jacobson:

104

It is clear the technological change enabled the steel industry to produce the same output with far fewer workers. Whether workers were displaced or not because of technical change is a more complicated question. Technical change may have led to relatively little job loss because most of the innovation represented replacement of existing equipment by major steel companies. These companies controlled the rate of introduction and were able to use their old labour force with the new equipment. There probably was some job loss, however, associated with the closing of old steel plants in areas where demand fell, such as Buffalo and Philadelphia.

In a novel approach to the question of technology and employment, Jacobson studied in detail how the *earnings* of displaced steel workers were affected. His findings were summarized as follows:

This paper was designed to measure how a fall in labour demand in the steel industry due to technological change, primarily the introduction of the Basic Oxygen Furnace, affected the earnings of steel workers.

A distinction is made between displaced workers, who would not have left except for the fall in demand, and other leavers, who are called attritions.

Measurements were made of the earnings losses of workers with different characteristics. Data used in the study were drawn from records maintained by the Social Security Administration. These records contained 15 year work histories of individual workers, including demographic information, employment, and earnings data.

In order to measure earnings losses the earnings of a group of workers who permanently left the steel industry in a particular year were compared with the earnings of a group of workers who did not leave in that year, using an autoregressive model of earnings determination.

The average loss due to displacement varies systematically with tenure and age. Low tenure workers have lifetime losses of about 4,000 1960-dollars. Losses increase with tenure, reaching a peak of $15,400 at about 15 years of tenure (about age 35).

To aggregate losses due to displacement in real and hypothetical cases, the number of displaced workers in each of nine age-tenure group is multiplied by losses estimated for that group and then summed across all groups. These displacement estimates were made as part of a larger study.

A typical result is that a 10% employment reduction would displace about 40,000 workers (out of a total labour force of 600,000) and the average loss per capita would be 7,700 1960-dollars.

It is more difficult in the case of the U.K. steel industry to relate technical change to levels of employment. This is because the government, via the nationalized British Steel Corporation, has provided huge subsidies which have maintained employment in unprofitable mills. However, because of the labour-saving nature of many steel industry innovations the U.K. industry, as in the U.S., has become more capital-intensive and less labour-intensive; from 1950 to 1973 the output of the British Steel Industry rose by 1.6 times, its real capital stock went up over three times and its employment fell by 27%. What can be stated with some certainty is that the growing uncompetitiveness of the British steel industry can be ascribed primarily to its relative technological backwardness. In the long term, it is this lack of *technical change competitiveness* which is liable to cost the U.K. industry most jobs.

Even in the West German steel industry, which is relatively highly efficient, between 500 and 1,000 jobs a month are being lost through rationalization in the face of world-wide overproduction. Since the 1974 recession, something like 40,000 jobs have been lost in the W.G. steel industry, and it is fear of unemployment that sparked off the recent steel strike in the Ruhr, the first for 50 years.

The steel-making Lorraine area of France is also threatened with rationalization and closures, which culminated in a recent riot by demonstrating steel workers in Paris. In the light of EEC policy, which plans for the loss of 200,000 jobs in the EEC steel industry over the next few years, this type of social unrest is likely to intensify.

The major problem of steel plant closure is one of concentration; that is, steel-making towns rely almost exclusively on local steel mills for male employment. As an example Corby, in the U.K., was virtually built around its steel works a generation or so ago. As a result of BSC rationalization plans, Corby is soon to lose 6,000 out of 11,000 steel jobs. The social consequences of this will be immense.

Summary

(a) Technical change has resulted in the loss of steel-making jobs in the U.S.A. and Europe.

(b) In the U.S.A., because of technical change, a constant output has been maintained since 1954 with much fewer workers.

(c) In the U.S.A. and Europe, many jobs have been lost through mill closures as a result of a fall in demand for steel (world-wide overproduction).

(d) In the long term, lack of technical change competitiveness poses the major threat to jobs in the steel industry, in the U.K. at least.

(e) Because the majority of male workers in steel-making areas in Europe rely on the steel industry for employment, mill closures cause severe social problems.

(f) The world recession, with accompanying fall in demand for steel, has resulted in world overproduction and consequent loss of employment, especially in less efficient steel plants. In this sense, fall in aggregate demand has made a major contribution to unemployment in the steel industry.

Remmerswaal (1978) has looked at the impact of production technology on employment in the metalworking industry.* Unlike the other cases presented in this section, his study is essentially forward looking.

Remmerswaal distinguishes three broad groups within this overall area, each of which is affected by technical development in different ways.

1. Production in large and very large quantities viz. cars, household appliances etc. These products as a rule are produced by large, capital-intensive industries of 5000 or more employees.
2. Production in small and medium lot-size numbers viz. capital-goods, instruments for industrial use, customer-made goods etc. In this group of products we shall look to factories of more than 50 employees.
3. In numbers circ. 70% of the industries are smaller than 50 employees. These industries are responsible for 20% of the workforce and are in general not capital intensive producers of individual customer-made products. Although there is a lot of change in these industries too, *we can consider them as a part of the services-industry*. The influence of technological development on the change in employment in this group is supposed to be of little importance. The total employment in absolute figures even tends to grow; in percentage of total employment it is bound to grow.

In the light of point 3 above, Remmerswaal limited his study to the first two groups of industries, representing roughly 30% of total firms and having about 80% of employment.

The mechanization of parts production has been established in the metalworking industry for many years, and mechanized

*Remmerswaal describes the metalworking industries as those making products or sub-assemblies for industrial or consumer use. This includes a good deal of the electro-technical, aero-space and off-shore industries. In the advanced Western economies these industries are responsible for between 25–30% of total manufacturing employment.

parts production has resulted in very high productivities coupled to increased quality of output. As part of this process labour has increasingly been displaced by machinery. Because of the complexity of assembly systems, and the complexity and amount of information necessary to run them optimally, however, it was not possible to transfer the relatively simple 'mechanization' type of automation to the automatic control of assembly lines. The development of the computer and associated means of very precise process control (e.g. robotics) means that the way is now open for automated assembly lines. More recent technological advances (e.g. microelectronics) have intensified this trend.

Remmerswaal distinguished four areas in which these technological advances will have a different influence:

1. Parts production in large and very large quantities. Beside the solved problem of the production information mechanisation we shall see a higher accuracy, reproducibility and higher outputs through adaptive control, automatic tool control and tool-changing resulting in shorter down-times.
2. Assembly in large and very large quantities becomes automatable through better and more reliable parts, computer controlled programmable robots, automatic sensing and group technology concepts. In the near future more use will be made of automatic fault diagnostics/fault-correction systems.
3. Parts production in small and medium lot sizes asks for flexible information processing. Production systems are developing, for parts grouped by group technology systems, recognizing the different parts and steering those automatically through the system in order to attain the different operations necessary.
4. The assembly in small and medium lot sizes will continue to use skilled labour, but the lead-times will be shortened by computer control of inventory control, materials management and more reliable parts resulting from automated parts production.

109

Based on these expectations, Remmerswaal discussed their influence on employment in the first two groups of factories mentioned earlier (large and very large quantities; small and medium batch).

Factories manufacturing products in large and very large quantities

There are a number of reasons why automation is feasible and possible in these factories:
1. constantly rising labour costs;
2. availability of skilled and unksilled labour for this type of work;
3. high absenteeism;
4. raising costs of recruiting and training people;
5. Unacceptability of monotonous, dangerous or unpleasant working conditions;
6. miniaturization, which changes production processes, and makes human work impossible and/or superfluous;
7. complex, high quality products which require a reliability of parts and sub-assemblies not reasonably to be expected of a human being.

Consequently there will be a further shift in the type of work in these factories to high quality maintenance people and more work for factories of the second group of industries. Our expectation is that by 1995 50% of the direct labour in automobile final assembly will be replaced by programmable automation. This happened in parts production in the automobile industry a long time ago.

Although there are no reliable overall figures available on employment in the electronics industries, it seems obvious that recent developments in large-scale integrated circuits result in comparable, or even greater, reductions in direct labour to produce the same functional possibilities. This type of industry can only survive economically in the Western World through automation which will render them comparable to process industries. The consequence of this will be a great reduction in direct labour, and *a different type of work for the remaining work force*. The speed of working will no longer be forced upon the operator by his machine: the operator will play much more of a controlling and supervising function in the process. This will result in higher levels of responsibility, higher skills and understanding of the consequences and more influence on technical and managerial decision-making.

Besides these changes, there will be more people involved in services to guarantee the smooth running of production, e.g. maintenance, inventory and production control, production planning, etc. This will generate jobs for better educated personnel, *who will have to be trained on the job* and who will need regular additional training to keep them abreast of developments in production engineering and their consequences for renovation and innovation in the product itself. This is in line with the expectation that by 1985 production-floor workers will be consulted as a matter of course on the structuring of any new jobs, or the changing of existing jobs, in at least 30% of the industries. They will also be consulted prior to plant environment changes in over 50% of the industries. By 1987 restructuring of all jobs will have taken place in at least 20% of the manufacturing industries and, as a consequence, each worker will be performing more work elements or complete operations instead of single, simple work elements.

Although all these changes seem to be revolutionary, the rate of change will be limited. Given a market for the ever increasing number of products per unit of time and per worker, and given the changing output of Western educational systems, there will be no drastic change in employment. A constant and slow decrease in the number of employees possessing a gradually increasing level of education may be expected. The forecasts are that by 1985 student work will be co-sponsored by companies and unions, so as to include hourly manufacturing experience in addition to the present practice of emphasizing staff work.

The expectations for 1990 for these industries are a 32-hour working week for a work force that on the shop floor will be

111

reduced by 50% and consist of people that are highly skilled and trained engineers and technicians. Their task will be to keep automated, robotized and computerized plants operating.

Factories manufacturing products in small and medium lot size numbers

Roughly 50% of metalworking employees work in factories ranging under this heading. It is here that the change in production technology and the application of computers will be much more dramatic: a strong rise in productivity can be expected without a comparable rise in demand: changes in information processing and organizational structure will result in roughly halving the indirect labour force. Quality assurance will influence the automation of parts production and change the amount of time spent in assembly, installation and maintenance.

In this type of industry the main problem has always been obtaining the right material and the right production information at the right time with the appropriately skilled man and his appropriate tools and machinery. Theoretically this problem is solvable today: it is a matter of developing the optimum information structure and the software to computerize information flows. Now the multi-accessible database and an understanding of group-technology systems are available, it can be expected that a radical change in these industries will take place. Group-technology and versatile computer-controlled production systems are greatly influencing parts production: through group technology the formation of work-cells becomes much more feasible, thus changing the work atmosphere on the shop floor, bringing job enrichment, and diminishing the amount of planning information on the one hand, and opening up the possibility of replacing the work-cell by a complete production system on the other.

As a result, work in progress will be greatly diminished as will lead-times. More reliable and constant quality can be expected and the *optimalization of production processes becomes less man-dependent*. The new infrastructure of production will demand higher levels of skill and education. Automation of the information flow will raise productivity and diminish the total work force requirement for the same production. In assembly the better quality and timing of the arrival of parts will result in a much higher productivity. As a consequence, increase in productivity of 200–300% might be expected. A consequent study of assembly in these factories will result in more standardization, better quality and even innovation in the products, etc.

In the next 5 years materials (composites) and forming capabilities will reduce the number of subassemblies in the final product. The much better organized information-flow is going to change the infrastructure of this branch. It is expected that within 10 years parts-storage and retrieval functions will become integrated automatically with manual or robotized assembly systems. Also the production-control function will be automated to the point that 80% of all-in process and finished inventory is controlled by a central computer. With a fairly static market for the goods produced by these factories, employment in the next 10–15 years will be roughly halved.

The viability of this expectation is underlined by the fact that in the next 10 years computer-aided design techniques will be adopted by 20% of these companies as an aid in designing parts and products to be assembled automatically. This will stimulate group technology in assembly resulting, by 1990, in its use in 50% of all assembly operations. Consequently, work will become more interesting, less monotonous, less dangerous and more integrated. In the next 10–15 years the output of these factories will double, or employment will decrease to roughly 50% of what it is today.

Summary

Remmerswaal summarized his deliberations as follows:
(a) Due to technological changes, under existing economic pressures, and given a continuity of the society of the Western world of today, a 30% reduction of employment in the next 10 years can be anticipated. In the following 10

years another 30% reduction of that work force can be expected, resulting roughly in a work force of 50% of that of today in 20 years. Tasks and functions will be quite different and the levels of skill and education will be higher.

(b) In general it can be said that the automation of the information-flow is the basis of process optimilization and roughly leads to a doubling of productivity. In the current industry there are large differences in the grade of automation or mechanization of the information needed. Therefore, the influence of the technological changes will differ from factory to factory. Great problems are to be expected in adapting the work force of today to the needs of tomorrow. Much time and money will be devoted by industry to train and retrain people in the next generation.

5(ix) NUMERICALLY CONTROLLED MACHINE TOOLS

The use of numerically controlled (NC) machine tools is increasing quite rapidly in all the industrially advanced nations. Since NC machines tend to have significantly greater productive capacities than the machines they replace (ratios of between 3:1 and 5:1 are reported), they might be expected to displace labour. Secondly, the additional production information available from machines that are linked to computers might be expected to enhance management control and thus cause some qualitative changes in workplace relationships. Finally, because they introduce a new technology into the workplace (electronics) they might be expected to dramatically alter maintenance skill requirements and to alter the requirements for traditional workshop skills.

A recent study in the U.S. of some 24 firms that were users of NC machine tools looked, among other things, at their manpower impact (Lund *et al.*, 1978). The most important findings of this study were:

— because most of the firms studied adopted NC machines at a time of substantial growth, even where their adoption led

114

to increased output this was not accompanied by a reduction in the workforce; displaced operators were simply absorbed into other areas of the shop;

— because of this, worker resistance to the use of NC machines was not as strong as it might have been under more adverse economic conditions;

— although it has been claimed that NC builds skill into the machine and hence requires less skill on the part of the operator, the study indicated a growing respect for the skills NC demands and a recognition that, although the operator does not need all the skills that are rquired to operate conventional machinery, a high level of mental alertness and the ability to act quickly in a crisis are required:

— the time necessary to train an NC operator is substantially shorter than that for conventional operator training (about 3 months and 14 months respectively);

— some supervisors who have been involved in traditional metalworking methods find the transition to NC disturbing. Lacking the intimate knowledge gained from actually operating NC equipment, they are more dependent on engineering staffs, maintenance people and parts programmers than in the past. This highlights the need for more effective supervisor and foreman re-training and skill-upgrading programmes;

— a major problem has been in the maintenance area. The problem is primarily one of diagnosing sources of failure. This may involve several specialists including the programmer, a mechanic, an electrician and an electronics technician;

— thus, the use of NC machine tools requires the firm to hire, or to gain access to, a range of new skills, notably programmers and electronics engineers;

— some NC manufacturers have, however, developed computer-based diagnostic skills (some operated remotely by data link over telephone lines, others installed at the plant location) which might reduce the requirement for in-house electronics skills;

— finally, a number of firms stressed that the additional production information (production output, machine downtime,

115

quality data) more easily available from machines linked to computers did enhance management control.

Swords Isherwood and Senker (1978(a)) studied the adoption of NC machine tools in workshops in the U.K. and West Germany. Among their major findings were:

— in both countries management resistance, and in particular resistance to undertaking new responsibilities, was more important than worker or trade union resistance in both the U.K. and W.G.;
— there was greater resistance to the use of NC machines in the U.K. and West Germany which was attributable mainly to the worse organization, training and education of British management.

A second study by the same researchers (Swords Isherwood and Senker, 1978(b)), this time of the changes in machines installed and workers employed in machine shops in the U.K. between 1971–72 and 1977–78, yielded the following results:

— one of management's principal motives for installing NC machines has been to maintain and increase production in the face of shortages of skilled labour;
— in general, the installation of NC machines has not affected overall manning patterns substantially. If certain types of conventional machine had been operated traditionally by skilled labour in a particular plant, this pattern of manning has been carried over to the operation of NC machines;
— the overall industry statistics confirm that there has been no dramatic change in the *proportion* of craftworkers employed;
— with the rapid recent increase in the use of NC machine tools it is no longer possible for machine shops to rely on manufacturers for maintenance. This means that the need exists for them to employ electronics maintenance specialists;
— NC machinery manufacturers are, however, taking advantage of recent technological advances in electronics to try to alleviate this problem;
— NC has created a need for programmers within the user companies;
— the use of NC equipment reduces the requirement for skilled

116

labour in fitting;

— management generally consider that skilled workers find the operation of NC machines boring, but semi-skilled workers appear to be less worried by this (the application in which NC machines are used might be critical in affecting this factor);

— the advent of microprocessor control systems provides management with the opportunity to build in more opportunities for shop-floor intervention to improve performance. Managements might, however, be reluctant to take advantage of this because it would lessen *their* opportunities for controlling output.

A major, and highly significant, conclusion of these researchers was that:

There has been a trend towards reduction in employment in the British engineering industry. Automation has played some part in causing this. But it has been the result to a greater extent of the failure of British management to invest sufficiently in research and development and production facilities to make products which would be more competitive on international markets. If management in the British engineering industry fails to remedy these deficiencies, the consequences in terms of job loss could be considerable because of the impact of overseas competition. If the industry does modernise, this could result in pressure to continue to reduce job opportunities. But the industry would be creating resources which collective bargaining can ensure are used to alleviate these effects by securing benefits such as shorter working weeks and better working conditions.

Summary

(a) The adoption of NC machine tools has not resulted in any great loss in employment in user firms, although the increased production capability conferred through the use of NC machines means a reduction in the requirement for new labour during periods of growth.

(b) The adoption of NC machines results in some craft de-skilling (in fitting and toolmaking, for example). At the same time it imposes increased skill requirements on managers and supervisors.

(c) Use of NC machines imposes a requirement for completely new skills, e.g. programming, electronics maintenance. Where firms cannot afford to employ such specialists on a full-time basis, the use of outside programmers and electronics technicians could represent a displacement of labour to the technical service sector.

(d) Computer-linked NC machinery enhances management control of the production process. Recent developments using microprocessors could, however, enhance worker control.

(e) While there was some worker resistance to the use of NC machines in the U.S. and Europe, this was relatively slight. In Europe resistance derived mainly from management.

(f) Some skilled workers experience a reduction in job satisfaction when using NC machines.

(g) In the U.K. the majority of jobs lost in NC machine user firms is due primarily to a lack of technical change competitiveness rather than job displacement through the adoption of the new technology.

5(x) COMPUTER-AIDED DESIGN

Backmann and Vahrenkamp (1978) have discussed the relationship between the service sector and the industrial sector. They consider that the differentiation of the industrial sector is a necessary prerequisite for the expansion of the service sector; it is only when the industrial sector expands strongly and is differentiated into very different branches that the demand for distribution, communication and related services increases. Further:

The close link between industrial sector and service sector is also exemplified by a process which might be called the 'service character of industrial productions'. What is meant by this is that the production of industrial goods is increasingly accompanied by services. On the one hand, this is due to the transfer of activities like transport, financing, insurance, advertisement, research etc. to specialised enterprises, which constitute an expanding field of social services. On the other hand, the demand for services such as advertisement, repair and official records increases steadily in the case of superior consumer goods.

Even today, the tendency emerges that the services offered become an integral part of the industrial product. If one considers these developments as a whole we find a strong dependence in the service sector on the growth of the industrial sector, which renders the dominance of the service sector in the long run very doubtful. . . . So far, it has been assumed in the literature that, in contrast to the industrial sector, it would be difficult to mechanise and rationalise the service sector, as these activities have a strong individual character and would therefore be difficult to unify to the extent that they can be handled by machines. With the increased use of electronic data processing (EDP), however, it became evident that a major share of these activities can be classified as information processing activities which can be mechanised by means of computers.

Rationalisation measures in the service sector can be roughly subdivided into three strategies of rationalisation: mechanisation, organisation and externalisation. Mechanisation is mainly effected by EDP, organisation by means of new patterns of organisation of work and externalisation via the nationalisation of services or through the transfer into the field of private work via the do-it-yourself movement. In the case of computer-aided design, the two strategies of mechanisation and organisation became effective.

Beckmann and Vahrenkamp consider the field of design as one of the planning of industrial production; thus, it can be

119

considered a service sector activity. There has been a rapid increase in the level of industrial design activity during the last 20 years, and it seems likely to continue to rise sharply in the foreseeable future. In the past this has led to considerable growth in employment in industrial design offices, mainly of engineers and draughtsmen. Whether the future growth in design activity will be accompanied by a similar growth in employment seems doubtful; rather, it seems likely that firms will resort to strategies of rationalization through mechanization.

One of the most notable features of design office work is the almost complete lack of machines: design work can therefore be considered as the manipulation of tools, which demands high manual skills, and as such it can be characterized as being artisan. The nature of design office work, however, renders it suitable for 'automation' using EDP systems, the so-called computer-aided design systems. To date, CAD has had only a minor impact on employment in the design office because the new technology has not yet been used extensively; Beckmann and Vahrenkamp, however, see CAD as being 'on the verge of broad diffusion'.

In West Germany alone there are currently about 500,000 persons employed in the design area. The widespread use of CAD will undoubtedly slow down the rapid increase in employment in industrial design; it might even reduce overall requirements. Thus on the macro-level, the occupational groups of technician, draughtsman and engineer have reduced possibilities for expansion than in the past.

The most far-reaching effects of CAD will, however, be qualitative rather than quantitative. First, the job content of the technical designer will be reduced in substance. Secondly, the handicraft-oriented, precision-mechanic activities of the draughtsman are devalued. Thirdly, the operation of the teletype console and the interpretation of the computer response on the screen become new fields of activity for the technical draughtsman. Teletype and screen activities, moreover, are general tools of the 'computer age' and not specific to the design department; hence, formerly highly *specific* skills are

120

becoming more *general* ones. As a result of these changes the technical draughtsman — a qualified professional requiring 3 years training — loses in importance. His training is replaced by a more demanding on-the-job training.

Summary

The activities of the designer — who is often a formally qualified engineer — are affected by the introduction of CAD in the following ways (some of these conclusions also apply to the technical draughtsman):

(a) In certain cases, specific engineering activities are completely automated.
(b) The framework for decisions concerning the design process is being determined by the computer and therefore becomes more restricted.
(c) The understanding of the content of the design tasks can no longer be left to the intuition of the designer, but has to be stated explicitly and precisely, and to be formalized.
(d) The planning medium of the designer changes from the conventional draft as iconic model of the design object, to symbolic and mathematical models which are less concrete and require an abstract understanding of the object. The thesis of the increasingly abstract nature of the job content is also confirmed by other surveys and has direct implications for a reorganization of professional training.
(e) The work process is organized on a more rigid time schedule. An economic use of the installations leads to a tendency towards day-work.
(f) The immediate work with the computer via the screen entails a great strain on the eyes and on the ability to concentrate. Beckmann and Vahrenkamp conclude: 'The work with computer terminals instead of with the drafting board appears to become the characteristic feature of the design activities. Some of our interview partners considered the rise of a new professional image of the engineer a realistic possibility. To this extent, a new profession of the computer-

aided designer could emerge if the educational and training system is flexible enough to adapt to these new requirements.'

(g) Finally, as a result of CAD, the demand for industrial design manpower will be reduced.

The subject of automation is vast, and it is beyond the scope of this book to offer even a brief summary. However, various aspects of the impact of automation on employment have already been covered in (vi), (vii), (ix) and (x) above. The possible impacts of the application of microprocessor technology on the employment effects of automation will be covered later (Chapter 7). In this chapter a number of employment related 'critical issues' associated with the automation of industrial processes will be discussed: the text is taken from a recent analysis prepared by Bernett *et al.* (1978) at MIT which distinguishes, among other things, the following four critical issues relating to employment:

1. Critical Issue

The human consequences of industrial automation extend beyond the impact on directly affected workers: the impact on supervisory, technical and managerial personnel increases with rising levels of automation.

Research on the effects of automation has been largely confined to the responses of workers directly affected by the installation of automated equipment and processes. The findings identify problems which fall under the classification of 'increased job dissatisfaction', as measured by such effects as employee attitude, increased absenteeism and turn-over. There is a substantial theme of resistance to change, raising the question of the true impact of automation — it is not clear from this literature whether the observed effects were the results of resistance to change regardless of source or the result of automation specifically.

The focus on the direct labour force leads to the implication that this is the only group within the firm which is affected by automation. However, as automaticity of the production process expands, the jobs of supervisory and managerial personnel begin to change. A manager's responsibilities may change from a mix of 40 people and 40 separate work stations to a complex of integrated equipment functioning as a single machine staffed by a handful of operators and supported by highly trained maintenance crews.

Not only will the nature of the supervisor's job change, but there may be serious questions about training, status and control. These uncertainties increase the likelihood that the supervisor will consciously or unconsciously resist the change in technology.

Managers are similarly affected: the managerial tasks and responsibilities in a highly automated environment *may differ* radically from those in a less 'automatic' productive system. While the manager's area of responsibility may remain essentially unchanged, the nature of the tasks and the technical content of the manager's job can shift dramatically. Also, the manager's perceived level of responsibility may have changed, producing new tensions.

2. Critical Issue

Automation can cause major change in the labour skill distribution required by an industrial firm: mobility and promotion opportunities may be severely restricted, 'freezing' some workers at the unskilled level and limiting the supply of internally trained workers at the highly-skilled level.

The concept of the division of labour — reducing each job to simple, repetitive tasks — is a fundamental notion underlying the Industrial Revolution. Today this concept is under attack as a basic source of worker alienation and job dissatisfaction. The concept was originally intended for application only to manual labour, yet the evolution of the factory system has gone hand-in-hand with increased division of labour at technical and supervisory levels. The impact of increasing automation on the division of human labour throughout the productive process is not yet clear: predictions range from dire forecasts of the reduction of human labour to animal-like machine-driven tasks to optimistic predictions of enlarged jobs increasingly under the control of the worker. Actual results to date suggest that both consequences can occur in the same location; the perception of the human impact will thus differ widely depending on the segment of the workforce observed.

A study recently completed by the Centre for Policy Alternatives found that the introduction of Numerical Control machine tools into metal-working can eliminate some moderately skilled jobs. Jobs requiring a higher level of skill — maintenance, programming, etc. — have been created, while skilled machine work has been replaced with 'machine-tending' tasks — parts feeding, material handling, tool changing [see (ix) above].

The new 'smart' technology may pose a new threat to long-term labour relationships. If a change in the distribution of labour skill requirements creates two distinct labour forces — an unskilled group at one end and a highly-skilled group at the other — the absence of moderately skilled, 'bridging' jobs would serve as a formidable barrier to upward mobility within the firm. The unskilled worker cannot acquire the experience and training on the job needed for a promotion to a highly skilled job, because the moderately-skilled intermediary job is not there. This raises the problem of the source of highly-skilled workers: the traditional opportunity for internal training along a path of increasing skills disappears. The firm must seek highly-skilled labour outside or develop a complete internal training program.

3. Critical Issue

Increasing automaticity of the physical technology can

cause restructuring of authority and control relationships in the organization; the appropriate organizational locus of effective human control of the productive process is a key design issue.

As in any goal-oriented system, a change in any part of a productive system can force changes elsewhere in order to maintain overall effectiveness. With orgainzational shifts the individual worker in a highly automated system may perceive his role as having no authority or control. Indeed, it is this characteristic of the work roles of people in automated settings that has attracted much research attention, and caused the most consternation among students of automation. Shepard has argued that automation as found in continuous process industries increases the worker's control and decreases the division of labour. The implication frequently drawn by other observers, however, is that, with substantial automaticity, there is no human control — the machines are in charge.

In fact, the authority and control over the productive process ultimately remains in the hands of human beings: there is some level and some location in the productive process where people exercise effective control. Conflicts arise when the level of control *shifts* during any change of organization or procedure. This fact is not likely to be recognized during the design stages of automation, but it may consequently be a major cause for difficulties during the start-up and operation.

There is the further problem of power relationships within an organization: 'information-based' power or 'knowledge-based' power can be taken from some and increased for others in an automated system. Changes — planned or otherwise — in an organization's power relationships tend to produce resistant behaviour. The process of automation is no exception. The nature of the physical technologies in highly automated productive systems is such that considerable technical skill may be required of the person fulfilling

125

the control function. For this reason, more engineers may find themselves in supervisory jobs. It is not necessarily the case, however, that a person trained in technology will have the supervisory and managerial skills for the control task.

4. Critical Issue

If the rate of application of automation and the consequent restructuring of the labour force advances faster than the nation's ability to cope with such change, the result may be a substantial permanent sector of unemployment in the labour force; such a sector would have important political and economic weight.

This critical socioeconomic issue is at the heart of much of the existing U.S. and foreign research and writing about the economic effects of automation. The problems posed by rapidly expanding industrial automation cannot be denied: there will be changes in the requirements for labour as firms move to restructure their operations towards increasing automaticity. The aggregate economic impact of these changes within firms will substantially affect the national economic picture, as well as the nation's place in the international economic community.

A recent OECD report cited in the *New York Times* has concluded that 'The evidence that we have is suggesting increasingly that the employment-displacing effects of automation, anticipated for the 1950's, are now beginning to arrive on a serious scale in the 1970's.' The report forecasts a period of 'jobless growth' in the 1980's in spite of expanded business investment. The governments of France and Great Britain, and a major company in West Germany have studies completed or underway to investigate the 'job-destroying potential of automation advances.' It is reasonable to conclude that, at present, the expansion of automation is out-pacing governments' ability to cope with the resulting changes in labour force requirements.

It is interesting to contrast this with a more optimistic view of the issue from the 1960's. In 1965 Dr. Yale Brozen of the University of Chicago concluded that '. . . the unemployment problem with which we are faced is not a result of automation and will not be worsened by automation. Automation should be welcomed as the means of alleviating poverty and undoing the damage done by bad wage laws and improper union–employer agreements. It should not be feared as a job destroyer. It is a job creator.'

At the heart of this issue is the question: should the burden of employment impacts of automation be borne by individuals, by firms, or by the nation? The way in which this question is resolved will substantially affect the future pace of industrial automation. If Congress were to conclude that public policy were best served by a slowdown in the growth of automation, restrictive legislation and regulation would result. However, should the government conclude that the nation's welfare were best served by increased automation, legislation and regulation (if any) might be directed towards mechanisms to ameliorate the impact on individuals affected by labour force changes.

In this political area the most serious danger is from poorly-informed public policy makers, swayed by political and economic pressure from a sector of the labour force which has been displaced by automation and which has no alternative means of returning to work. In the absence of good information there is danger that public policy thus formed might actually exacerbate the problem, rather than remedy it.

The situation today is sufficiently serious to warrant immediate and careful attention. As the OECD report indicates, there is already evidence of the development of an 'automation-induced' sector of the unemployed labour force. We contend that this sector will in fact become a permanent fact of life: as automation expands, there will be a constant 'inventory' of people who have been displaced because of automation. The nature of this 'inventory' will be defined by answers to these critical questions:

— what will be the aggregate size of this 'inventory' of people,

127

- how rapidly can this 'inventory' be turned, and
- will the newer forms of automation (robotics, computer control) actually cause a permanent reduction in the labour force, so one part of the 'inventory' consists of those no longer employable by industry?

Clearly, if this sector becomes a growing pool of the permanently displaced, it would become a politically powerful anti-automation block. But, if this sector is instead a rapidly turning over pool of temporarily displaced workers, automation will be a lesser threat to individual security. The probability of political action will be considerably reduced.

Summary

The above abstracts from the MIT report have clearly summarized, in a general sense, a number of the employment-related issues which emerged from the more specific case studies presented in this section. Among the most significant factors highlighted by the MIT researchers are:

(a) Automation gives rise to increased job dissatisfaction among shop-floor workers.
(b) Automation gives rise to significant changes in the technical content of managerial tasks.
(c) Automation can result in some de-skilling and the creation of new, higher level skills.
(d) Automation can reduce upward job mobility prospects for some unskilled workers.
(e) Automation can significantly alter the power and control relationships within an organization.
(f) Unless automation generates increased output and wealth and results in growth in aggregate demand, it might result in structural unemployment.

128

A summary of the impact of technical change on employment in the ten sectors covered in this chapter is given in Table 5.13.

The greatest impact on employment through technical change so far has taken place in the agricultural sector. The application of mechanization in addition to advances in herbicides, fertilizers, husbandry and plant breeding, not only made a large percentage of the agricultural workforce redundant, but has also virtually destroyed the need for certain widespread skills associated with the use of horses. At the same time, however, it created the need for new skills associated with the operation and maintenance of machinery. It also created the need for professional farm management.

The use by manufacturing firms of numerically-controlled machine tools appears to have had only a marginal impact on *levels* of employment to date. Their greater productive potential has, however, enabled companies to expand output with existing labour forces (jobless growth). A similar effect was seen in the U.S. steel industry, where output was maintained with a much-reduced workforce. The major source of job loss in capital goods — in a number of European countries at least — has been lack of technical change competitiveness; this has been clearly apparent in a number of specific industry sectors.

In most instances the adoption of new manufacturing technology has meant some de-skilling in certain craft areas, and the generation of new, higher level skills. In the case of automation, the demarcation lines between previously specific skills have been destroyed and new, *polyvalent* jobs have been created. Automation has also affected the pattern of control of manufacturing processes in that control has become increasingly centralized. The perceived *quality* of work has also been affected by the use of automated and semi-automated machinery, which has resulted in some job dissatisfaction among skilled workers whose specialized job function has been partially replaced by numerical controls. Automation has also meant the partial replacement of traditional apprentice-

129

Table 5.13. *Summary of the Quantitative and Qualitative Impacts of Technical Change on Employment in a number of Industries*

	Agriculture	Coal mining	Canadian Railways	Textile Machinery	Textile Industry	Cement Industry	Steel Industry	Metalworking Industry	NC machine tools	Computer-aided design	Automation
Reduction in labour force	√	√			√		√	√			
Increased output with same or reduced labour force (jobless growth)	√	√	√		√		√	√	√	√	√
De-skilling or making certain skills redundant	√		√		√	√			√	√	√
Generated the need for new skills	√	√	√	√	√	√		√	√	√	√
Reduction in job satisfaction					√			√	√		√
Required higher level management skills	√	√		√	√	√		√	√	√	√
Displacement of specialist skills outside the factory					√	√			√	√	
Job loss due to lack of technical change competitiveness				√			√		√		

ships with increased on-the-job training.

The adoption of new machinery embodying electronic controls has imposed the need on firms to displace certain skills outside the factory, e.g. maintenance and software specialists, and has thus resulted in greatly increased sub-contracting. Recent developments in computer technology mean that some functions (fault diagnosis) will be increasingly incorporated in the control system itself.

A number of factors were evident which either accelerated or retarded the adoption of new labour-saving technology. For example, in the pre-war years an abundance of cheap labour and conservative union practices retarded the mechanization process in the U.K. coal mining sector. In the textile industry, postwar technical change accelerated because of a paucity of skilled labour. In both the textile and coal mining industries competition forced the pace of technical change, in the first case competition from cheap labour cost countries, in the second case competition from cheaper forms of energy.

In some areas resistance to change has derived mainly from management, e.g. NC machine tools. In other areas, e.g. coal mining, worker resistance to mechanization was brought about through lack of adequate preparation on the part of management. In fact, in most areas, the successful adoption of new technology has imposed greater skill requirements on management and has increased the need for managers to acquire technical skills.

In the past, there does not appear to have been a great deal of vigorous worker resistance to technical change. However, much of the change described in this section occurred at a time of increased aggregate demand for manufactured goods, and a high rate of growth in the service sector. With current high levels of unemployment and a stagnating world economy, this situation is liable to change. This is evidenced by the recent strife in the steel industries in France and West Germany.

An extremely important factor in adapting to the employment impact of technological change — which was highlighted in the study of Canadian Railways — is the time it takes for the

131

new technology to displace the old. In the case of Canadian Railways, replacement was gradual, which greatly facilitated the labour readjustment process. One of the current fears concerning the use of microelectronics is the potential speed with which the readily available technology might replace existing plant. If this process is too fast, insufficient time will be available to properly re-train and reorganize both labour and management to enable them properly to adjust to the change. In this case, it might be that the major barrier retarding change will be worker and/or management reaction.

CHAPTER 6

THE IMPACT OF MICROELECTRONICS ON EMPLOYMENT

Much of the current concern about the employment impact of technology is based on the belief that the widespread adoption of new microelectronically-controlled plant and equipment will result in job displacement on a relatively massive scale. Moreover, in the case of microelectronics there are two factors which intensify this concern: the first is the speed with which (currently available) microelectronics-based technologies might diffuse throughout the economy; the second is the widely-held belief in the potential of microelectronics devices to displace labour in the services sector, especially the office worker (as pointed out in Chapter 3 of this report, the service sector has been largely immune from 'technological unemployment' effects and has, in fact, been the major source of employment growth during the post-Second World War era).

Maddock (1978) has summed up the main ways in which the 'microelectronics revolution manifests itself':

1. By its ability to extend or even displace man's capacity for thinking, his intuition or his judgement.
2. By its pervasiveness; there is virtually no field in manufacturing, the utilities, the service industries or commerce that can fail to be influenced by this advance — very likely in a profound manner.
3. Replacing many devices which have traditionally been the territory of precision mechanical (or electromechanical) devices by purely electronic systems — itself a very sub-

stantial revolution. Cash registers, wrist watches, telephone exchanges, etc., have already gone this way, many more will follow.

4. The speed of advance. Never has a powerful technology advanced so rapidly in such a short time. The performance of single chip measured in terms of the gates it can contain (see Fig. 6.1) has increased ten thousandfold in a period of 15 years. The speed of obsolescence of not only the chips themselves but of all the ways they can be applied is so great that there has hardly been time to get adapted to one regime before another emerges.

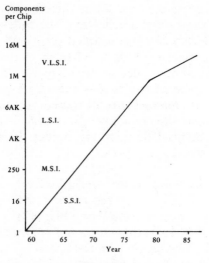

Figure 6.1.

5. Reduction of cost. Not only has the performance increased, but even more remarkable has been the reduction of cost. Fig. 6.2 shows that in a period when inflation and escalating costs are the norm, the price of each unit of performance has reduced one hundred thousandfold since the early 1960s.

6. Reliability. Already the reliability of the semi-conductor devices far exceeds that of any engineering device to date and

134

it continues to improve.

7. Flexibility. Because microprocessors are programmable their performance can be changed quickly and cheaply — as distinct from all earlier engineering products.

Clearly the impact of microelectronics on employment is likely to be considerable. However, it would be a pity if only the potentially negative employment aspects of the use of electronic controls were emphasized here. Meadows (1978) pointed to the role that electronic controls can play in alleviating problems caused by skilled labour shortages in buoyant industries: 'In Seattle, where Boeing is tripling its output of

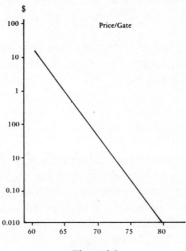

Figure 6.2.

747's and beginning production of new models, the expansion has been paced to the availability of skilled labor. Boeing has cut its need for skilled labor by using a computer-controlled mechanism that selects wiring and assembles it for installation in the fuselage. Computer-controlled drills, moving on caterpiller tracks, bore holes automatically.'

This raises the more general question of production efficiency

135

and its relationship to competitiveness: failure to introduce microelectronically-controlled manufacturing sequences through fear of immediate loss of jobs will result in lack of international competitiveness with subsequent catastrophic employment effects; thus, it will simply be a matter of weighing short-term unemployment against long-term survival.

By no means all applications of microelectronics are labour displacing. A growth in demand for new microelectronically-controlled industrial processes will lead to a general growth in the industries supplying them. The development and manufacture of a whole new generation of 'smart' producers will result in growth of new firms to manufacture them. Once again, however, failure to utilize the new technology will lead to lack of technical change competitiveness with subsequent national job loss.*

The remainder of this section presents an outline of the current and/or future impact of microelectronics on a number of sector and technologies.

6(i) WATCH-MAKING INDUSTRY

During the past decade or so the world's watch-making industry has undergone a technological revolution, with mechanical controls being replaced first by a quartz oscillator coupled with a specially designed frequency-reducing circuit, and then a quartz oscillator coupled with a general purpose microprocessor. In less than 10 years some 45% of world-wide production of watches switched to electronics.

Commenting on this electronics revolution, Barron and Curnow (1979) point out: 'At the national level the impact on employment and international trade has been large. For example, some 20–30% of the assembly labour in Switzerland

---

*For example, there is some evidence to suggest that Japanese and U.S. firms, producing advanced NC machine tools based on the use of microprocessor controls, are beginning to pose a threat to West German firms whose more conventional machinery currently dominates OECD markets.

was displaced, resulting in federal intervention for the first time, and trade estimates suggest a swing in balance of payment of at least $250 million per annum.'

Freeman and Curnow (1978) suggest that the electronic revolution in watch making illustrates certain features which may be repeated in other areas:

1. Total disbelief by established watch assemblers and their suppliers in the potential of the new technology, citing prestige, quality, protected outlets with high margins, marketing know-how, absence of appropriate repair and maintenance facilities as barriers.
2. Savage price competition between suppliers of electronic watches, accompanied by technical innovation adding more facilities as simple products saturated the market.
3. Completely new cost-volume elasticities through all stages of manufacture, accompanied by the opening of new markets with new price-volume elasticities.
4. Different skill embodiments at all stages from design through manufacture and assembly to marketing, and to new product succession.
5. Relocation of different. stages of watch production internationally, with considerable (i.e. greater than $200m) swings in balance of payment for individual countries.
6. Despite a once-and-for-all increase in market volume, a diminution in total market turnover, accompanied by an overall drop in labour required.
7. Decreased economic activity in previous outlets and associated facilities, accompanied by a lesser increase in new outlets and facilities.
8. A differential impact of these consequences, particularly as far as production is concerned, between countries.

Freeman and Curnow go on to point out that: 'A similar pattern of issues and consequences can be seen in the pocket calculator market, where contrary to popular belief, an older electromechanical product — the desk calculator — has been totally displaced.'

Clearly, the adoption of microelectronics in watch manufacture caused a major shift in employment between countries, from those heavily committed to mechanical systems (e.g. Switzerland) to those vigorously applying the new technology (e.g. Japan). A similar pattern occurred in the calculator industry.

Finally, while there appear to have been few market barriers to the acceptance of digital watches, there were management barriers to the adoption of the new technology in firms manufacturing mechanical watches. These management barriers took the form primarily of complacency, and a general disbelief in the market potential of the new technology. This might have been based on total ignorance of the nature of microelectronics on the part of management.

6(ii) WORD PROCESSING AND AUTOMATION IN THE OFFICE

In the words of an IBM sales brochure, word processing is 'the simplification and improvement of traditional typing, secretarial and clerical functions through a managed system of people, procedures and modern office equipment'. Since the 1920s the introduction of the accounting machine and more recently the computer have transformed large areas of office practice; the use of technology in the office is, therefore, nothing new. What is new about word processors is that they affect the type of office work known as secretarial which, up to now, has been little affected by technology. The development of this new range of microelectronics-based products which are intended to replace the typewriter has great potential to radically alter the performance of secretarial tasks.

Before discussing the impact of word processors on clerical employment, it is worth while considering the impact computers have had on employment in the service sector. A recent report by the Central Policy Review Staff (1978) has commented on the employment impact of computers in the U.K. Civil Service:

138

The predictions about employment that are now being made about microelectronics were being made twenty or so years ago about earlier generations of computers. The Civil Service has used computers for a number of years and a study of the employment effects shows how wrong those predictions were.

The justification for the use of computer systems rather than manual systems has been heavily dependent upon the staff savings they are said to make possible. An example of this is the computerised payment of unemployment benefit. By 1977/78 some 1,650 (mainly clerical) posts had been saved (partly offset by some 450 computer related posts). This picture is repeated in other computer installations, but taking a wider view there has between 1970 and 1977 been a growth from 170,000 to 200,000 staff in categories most likely to have been affected by computer installations.

The reasons for this paradox (the more the computers, the more the staff) are not hard to find. In some cases the computer applications have themselves suggested new areas of work and new services that Government Departments could develop with benefit to the community; in other cases the staff freed by computer applications have been absorbed in new services (not of themselves computer related) which could not have been developed at all had computers not freed them. In 1977 the numbers of staff actually engaged in computer operations was about 14,000 and the numbers 'freed' by computers were several times that figure. Yet the total numbers employed in the areas affected had risen significantly. In short, the conclusion is that the employment effect of computers in the Civil Service has been at best to restrain the growth of clerical employment and certainly not to reduce it.

Total U.S. office costs in 1977 were $441 billion, of which 84% was labour, 10% office equipment and 6% electronic data processing (EDP). Clearly with this cost structure, there is great scope for the reduction of labour costs via the use of the new microprocessor-based office systems, and indeed there are

139

something of the order of 350,000 word processing machines currently in use in the U.S.

It is of particular importance to note that the majority of the people employed as secretaries or typists are women and, indeed, typing has been one of the major growth areas of female employment and the need for typists has greatly contributed to the ability of women to obtain independent employment. Thus, the development of word processing seems likely not only to have a considerable impact on the overall size of the clerical work force, but also to have a particular critical importance for working women.

Simply because this new technical capability exists does not, however, mean that it will enjoy immediate and widespread adoption, and McLean and Rush (1978) have listed a number of barriers to the adoption of world processors:

Having established both the potential for technical change and the social importance of such change for the office environment it is interesting to note that, in general, market forecasts (made by equipment suppliers) that the market was about to take off in a big way have been an annual occurrence for the last 3 or 4 years and have (at least in the UK) up to now been proved wrong. Though it has been almost universally recognised that office procedures have been ripe for mechanisation — growing costs and numbers of office staff, increasing volumes of paper work, low capital investment per worker compared with manufacturing industry — it would nevertheless seem that the perception of the potential of the productivity gains have been outweighed at least in the UK by the inertia of traditional practices in all but the largest organisations. Such conservatism is by no means irrational for there are a number of features of word processing systems which tend to slow down the rate of acceptance by businessmen. One of these has been a quite sensible concern that the sophisticated electronics incorporated in word processing systems might prove less reliable than the essentially mechanical technology of conventional typewriters. The

140

business man's acceptance of the risk involved in adopting the new technology have also not been counterbalanced by novel methods of marketing by word processing equipment manufacturers, word processing equipment is still mostly sold or rented. It is significant to recall that the diffusion of the penultimate generation of copying equipment was greatly facilitated by the novel marketing approach adopted by the Xerox corporation, copying machines were neither sold nor rented but instead a flat rate charge was levied upon each copy made. It would seem likely that word processing equipment would be more readily accepted if the risks involved, as in the case of the xerographic copier were born initially by the manufacturers and not by the users.

Another drawback in the rapid take up by industry of modern word processing systems consists of the series of complex interrelated problems concerned with the legality and security of business information and correspondence. For example, at present the law requires that copies of binding written contracts should be identical for all the contracting parties; whereas few high speed printers incorporated in word processing systems are capable of producing multiple identical copies, most can only produce sequential copies and the legal validity of such copies is in doubt. Such apparently minor legal problems are highlighted by the extremely futuristic claims of equipment manufacturers whose sales literature is often focused around such concepts as 'the paperless office'; current legal and ethical business requirements still depend very heavily on the need for apparently 'objective' paper records of business transactions. Many potential users of word processing systems may possibly be deterred by the thought that many written communications may never appear as hardcopy on paper and feel that the security and privacy of business communications may be threatened by the new technology.

All the above barriers to the diffusion of microelectronic technology in the office can be regarded as aspects of a transition problem. In common with many examples of radical technical change word processing equipment would seem to work best in an environment where the whole *system* of office work has been reconsidered and transformed. Few British manufacturers of word processing equipment or indeed few office mangers in the UK are willing or capable of assessing office work on a total system of inter-related tasks. The ability, for the business man, to view the complete office work load as a system has no inherent geographical boundaries; although, of course, office management in some countries seem to be more capable of accepting this idea than the managements of other countries.

There might be other barriers which are sociological in nature, namely that managers enjoy having a personal secretary (often a confidante), and particularly like the status which having a secretary confers on them.

A logical extension to the use of word processors, and one which seems feasible in the light of developments in microelectronic technology, is the *automated office*. Barron and Curnow (1979) have discussed, in some detail, the effects of automation on office organization and employment:

There are over 1,000,000 secretaries and typists in the UK. There are a further 750,000 involved in administrative work and a further 400,000 in management. The advent of the automated office will affect the way all these people work, by changing the pattern and efficiency of information flow.

The electronic typewriter enables an improvement in productivity and could lead to a direct reduction of labour in typing pools. The functions of a secretary are far more diverse and although the electronic typewriter, and more importantly other aspects of the automated office will improve her efficiency, this may not lead to a proportional reduction in the level of staffing. In the first place the position of a secretary is a status symbol which will not be given up readily; secondly, secretaries are distributed throughout an organisation making it more difficult to eliminate individual posts, even if they are underutilised.

The major change will only come if the electronic typewriter is effective as a working tool for management itself. If this happens, then the use of a secretary as an intermediary becomes unnecessary, and the large reductions in staffing levels will be possible. Where the electronic typewriter provides other facilities of direct benefit to the manager, for example access to personalised data processing capability, this barrier may be broken down rapidly. Otherwise, the difficulty of typing and the question of status will keep the electronic typewriter firmly in the outer office.

The introduction of direct speech input would change this situation completely. With direct input, the secretary not only becomes unnecessary, but is a direct obstacle to the effective use of the electronic typewriter. Direct speech input is, therefore, expected to have a far more radical effect on the pattern of office work and the level of employment of secretaries than the first stage of the automated office.

Direct voice input is regarded as a difficult problem and in spite of repeated predictions and announcements to the contrary, it is not expected to become practical in the short or medium term.

Office automation must be expected to have a radical impact on the efficiency of information flow within a company. This in turn may be expected to have an effect on the overall efficiency of the company, particularly in the way it utilises resources, and hence on its competitiveness. Much of management activity is concerned not with decision making, but with the collection and distribution of information. The development of the automated office may, therefore, also be expected to affect the functions of mangement and indirectly provide a substantial improvement in the manager's efficiency. Thus, office automation may be expected to reduce the number of managers required to operate a company (and thereby to generate a further reduction in the secretarial requirements).

Finally, there is the management consultancy effect. Much

143

of the improvement in efficiency arising from the introduction of data processing, came not from the computer itself, but from the opportunity to examine procedures critically and to change them when data processing was introduced. Much the same pattern may be expected with the introduction of office automation.

The introduction of office automation may be expected to lead to high levels of unemployment in secretarial, typing, administrative and management staff, and as such, it might be expected to lead to a complex of social changes. Unlike other aspects of automation (data processing, factories) the sectors of employment under threat are not the general work force but the administrative force with the emphasis predominantly on female workers. Thus any displacement would have major social consequences for female independence and family income. At present there is high job mobility and a low level of unionisation, so that initially, at least, the work force would be unable to resist the pressures. Management has shown a similar pattern of fragmentation and inability to exert social pressures (for the same reason, because there has been no need). Under the threat of unemployment it might be expected that both sectors will become more organised and militant. The consequences could be far reaching, creating the opportunity for greater strife between the main sectors of the community.

The adoption of office automation could have a further social consequence. Office workers are highly concentrated into the civil service, local government and the major towns. Thus any unemployment will not only be distributed non-uniformly across the population but also geographically, and between the public and private sectors.

Office automation is seen as having far greater social and economic impact than any other aspect of the information revolution, and must be the primary problem to be addressed by any Government policy.

It would seem therefore that it is not the worker in the shop floor who has the most to fear from the computer, but the office worker and his manager. The impact of information technology, even on a major manufacturing company like British Leyland, will be greater on the office staff than on the assembly line. In fact, British Leyland employs more in office staff and management than those in direct manufacture. Not only are the number of employees involved greater but a greater gain in productivity is almost certainly possible by improving the efficiency of the office rather than the efficiency of the production line.

In the light of the above discussion on the potential employment impact of microelectronics in the office, it is worth while recording that there exists some evidence to suggest that the use of word processors can have a *positive* impact on office employment. Branscomb (1978), in a recent lecture, stated that IBM's experience was that employment was slightly increased in offices using word processors, and that the secretary's job content was broadened and job satisfaction increased. Parkinson (1978) reported similar findings; in the U.S. experience office staff increased by a factor of 1.2 and, due to greater output capability using word processes, it was possible for the secretary to handle a greater variety of duties and more complex tasks.

Finally, the Central Policy Review Staff Report (1978) commented on these issues as follows:

> Word processors are microprocessor-based typing systems. Work measurement experiments seem to point fairly consistently to productivity gains something in excess of 100 percent, comparing word processors with conventional typewriters. Thus, in theory, they should make it possible for organizations which employ them to reduce their employment of typists by more than 50 percent. In practice this has not occurred. Many organizations have invested in word processors in order to assist them in overcoming shortages of typists, and organizations often discover that word processors

145

make possible new ranges of services — the use of standard letters as prestige forms of advertizing — to which they attach more value than they do to the potential staff saving. Thus in a way which is in some sense analogous to the experience of the Civil Service with computers, the potential productivity does not translate at all directly into actual job loss.

It might be, therefore, that while word processors will have only a marginal impact on *current* levels of office employment (at least in the short term) their greater productivity will enable firms to increase office workloads with existing staff. Thus, *future* employment prospects are affected and a pattern of 'jobless growth' might well be established in this aspect of the service sector.

6(iii) MICROELECTRONICS IN THE PRINTING INDUSTRY

There has been a great deal of publicity recently about the employment effects of new microelectronics-based control systems on the printing industry. According to a recent article in the *Financial Times*, every aspect of the business is changing with the impact of electronics technology. In the studios the latest scanning equipment automatically prepares complex layouts with the wave of a light pen, and microprocessors are making their first appearance in press and ink controls. Binding lines too are becoming automated. *In each case the developments mean lower manning levels and require less skill from the operator.*

It is in photosetting that the most dramatic changes are occurring. There are systems available for every user, large and small, but the impact of word processing on the printer's typesetting will be even more significant when it occurs.
Already word processing equipment is being interfaced with typesetters, and office equipment is improving in quality to match the output of the traditional printer.

A notable feature of this new potential, at least in the U.K., has been vigorous worker resistance to the new technology. A second article in the *Financial Times*, under the heading 'Unions keep a watchful Eye on New Technology' states:

Events on the labour front in Fleet Street and in the general print industry over the past couple of years have shown the difficulties which management face in persuading printers and their unions to accept the introduction of new technology in the face of printers' concern about the human and social consequences of the change. This industry has not had a serious national stoppage since 1959 when there was a six-week strike over pay. This year, however, this industry has been rocked by a major battle at Times Newspapers over new technology in Fleet Street. But it has shown a determination to ensure that its members obtain as much financial reward as possible from the advance of the new technology into the industry. Pride in the old crafts has no doubt played its part in fanning feelings of insecurity and mistrust in the industry.

Barron and Curnow (1979) have commented on the adoption, in the U.K. newspaper industry, of computerization:

The pattern of computerization being adopted was by no means the latest technology, but represented a logical evolution of computerization advancing piecemeal over a wide range of activities, though still 10 hears behind potential. The new technology offered working conditions cleaner, quieter and simpler than the displaced technology. The displaced technology was considerably over-manned, and the new technology would require less manning anyway.
    Although the headquarters of the various unions involved had, in negotiation with the employers, agreed generous redundancy terms, the unions involved, at a local level, rejected those proposals. In inspection it became clear that the proposed national solution did not tackle the issue of the re-distribution of jobs under the new technology. The basic

147

problem is that the new pattern of skills cannot be mapped onto the previous pattern of skills, and that the previous pattern of skills had clearly defined internal boundaries associated with different unions. Additionally, regarded as a flow process, the evolution of unions had been such that their roles appeared at multiple points in the production flow.

The union members concerned were quite informed as to the long-term potential threats to the newspaper industry, and were quite aware that full acceptance of the new technology would diminish their leverage since the new process was less multiplestep, and less time consuming. Additional anxiety was expressed about the disappearance of craft skills, and control of entry into the industry.

Barriers in this case were solely inter- and intra-union anxiety about the reallocation of jobs to workers in the absence of clear cut criteria. The high wages demands are not high in relation to the system economics — a consequent barrier may well be the public attitude that the print unions are bloody-minded, and the resultant stiffening of attitudes.

The above, rather dismal picture of resistance to change is by no means universal in the newspaper industry, and Stark (1978) has described how the Providence, Rhode Island, *Journal Bulletin* successfully gained worker acceptance for the new printing technology.

The area in which it seems to be generally agreed that the Journal-Bulletin is the leader in the field is in our settlement with composing-room employees whose jobs were phased out by the new technology. In 1971 we employed 242 persons there: now there are 98; by 1980 we are scheduled to have only 54. The company proposed an extremely generous 'incentive reduction' plan of money and benefits which Al Aleixo, president of the Providence Typographical Union, says is far superior to what any other paper in the nation has offered its employees.

148

Under the current agreement, all employees between the ages of 62 and 65 who agree to retire early (mandatory retirements is age 65) are eligible for a 'voluntary displacement bonus' of $500 for each year of continuous service or fraction of a year, with a minimum of $20,000. These employees also get $250 a month until age 65 or date of death, whichever is soonest, and paid medical and life insurance until age 65.

Employees between the ages of 50 and 62 are eligible for the displacement bonus, with certain modifications; a weekly payment up to age 62 of half a week's pay, and then the $250-a-month payment from age 62 to 65; and paid medical and life insurance to age 65.

Employees under age 50 have a number of choices: the displacement bonus plus relocation expenses anywhere in the country; the bonus plus interest-free loans up to $10,000 for business ventures; tuition up to $5000 a year for four years if they are attending a university, plus $800 a month living expenses while they are enrolled, plus relocation expenses; or the bonus plus tuition up to $5000 a year for two years if they attend a trade school or junior college and $800 a month living expenses while they are enrolled, and relocation expenses.

'The company came to us when they decided they wanted to bring in the computers', recalls Aleixo, 'and said, Here's what we want to do. They took us to the computer companies and showed us what the future looked like. We realised that we could dig in our heels and fight this every step, or we could work hand in hand with the company and get the best possible settlement for our people, and I think we've done that.'

Of the composing-room employees who have left, most have simply retired. About a dozen have opened their own businesses: print shops, a bar, a motel in Florida, a bicycle-repair shop, a coin laundry, a home-heating-oil supply firm. About 16 are attending trade schools or universities in subjects as diverse as aviation, forestry, auto mechanics, business management and design. Others have found jobs as cooks, house painters or computer technicians.

Perhaps most interesting of all, five are now reporters, one is a photographer and three are advertising salesmen for the Journal-Bulletin, under a special retraining programme. I work directly with the reporters and photographer and can say that they hold their own with the rest of the staff.

They have the particular admiration of others in the news-room: we can appreciate the risk taken by men in their 30s and 40s with families to support in ending one career and taking up something very different, knowing they'd be com-peting in many instances with either younger, university-educated reporters, or with seasoned veterans. They do well and seem to enjoy their new jobs. Clearly the VDTs have made it possible to produce some sort of newspaper with fewer people overall, and implicit in that statement is the understanding that, in a strike, it would be far easier than ever before for supervisory personnel to get a paper out. Even if local reporters refused to work, a few editors could fill up the paper with wire copy, and composing-room supervisors could paste it up. You may debate for yourselves what this does to the effectiveness of strikes in the future, but electronics doesn't have to be perverted into a union-buster. As the Journal Company's agreement with the typo-graphical union has shown, there are satisfactory — but not cheap — settlements to be reached with those whose jobs are phased out. When you walk into our newsroom now, it's a lot quieter than it used to be. There's very little clattering and clanking of typewriter keys; now there's the muted click of the computerised keyboards. The terminals, with their constantly-flashing cursors, wink like giant eyes. The com-posing room is still: the Linotypes and metal chases are gone, replaced by cold type and wax. Our vocabularies are differ-ent. To the journalistic jargon now add computer slang: 'Do a QI on that, H&J it and then Qs to CMPDON and purge it', which is just another way of saying, 'Find that story, where-ever it is. Tell me how long it is. Then get rid of all the type from yesterday's paper'. We are not only reporters and editors any more; we are technicians and typesetters and trail-blazers. I wonder what newspapers will be like in another 50 years.

Other areas of the printing industry are also being affected by the new technology, and once again worker resistance has manifested itself because of changes in both the numbers and nature of jobs involved. A recent article by Goodacre (1979) has shown, however, how the adoption of microprocessor-controlled inking systems can have a positive impact on both efficiency and employment in individual firms. Commenting on the firms of Reiff & Co. of Offenburg, Goodacre states: '. . . investment in new technology resulting in an actual 10 per cent per annum increase in staff during recent years. Turnover has increased at the same time by 20-25 per cent. . . . Additionally it is claimed that Reiff minders are producing 50 per cent more output through reduced downtime. . . . Even though it is only early days the signs are that a doubling of productivity is on the cards plus a dramatic increase in overall quality.'

Thus, through the use of the new technology, higher quality and efficiency have improved Reiff's production capacity and competitive position and have enabled the firm to generate greater employment.* The message here is clear and is that in the highly competitive world of printing, failure to adopt the new technology will lead to a decline in market share with a consequent fall in employment; in the more progressive firms, on the other hand, increased quality and efficiency will result in increased turnover and the generation of new jobs. It seems, however, likely that the *global* demand for employment in the printing industry will, as a result of the new technology ultimately decline, and that the nature of the skills required in the printer's job will inevitably change.

---

*The new technology also meant that there was a requirement for new skills, namely an electronics technician.

There seems little doubt that the use of microelectronics will radically alter manpower requirements in telecommunications, both in the producer and user industries. At the same time both the efficiency and the range of services should increase significantly.

Wilkinson (1978) has commented on the role of technical change in reducing manpower requirements in the U.K. telecommunications industry:

> As the old electro-mechanical gear is phased out, whole factories have been closed and many thousands of jobs have disappeared. In 1973, the telecommunications industry employed 90,000 people. By 1976, it was down to 75,000 and it is now around 65,000.
>
> This trend will continue as complicated mechanical swtiches are replaced by electronic circuits which can often be assembled automatically. Indeed, the reduction in jobs in the purely manufacturing side of the business could be startling. Dr. Corfield of STC says that after the electronic TXE4 exchange, the next stage of switching technology (System X) will require only a tenth of the present number of production workers as exchange equipment is reduced to a 15th of its present size.
>
> Looking ahead, he says: 'The next ten years should see a thousandfold increase in capability per unit volume.' However, skilled designers, computer programmers and engineers will probably be needed in greater numbers.

Some of these changes are illustrated schematically in Figure 6.1.

In terms of the user, it has been suggested that there will be great qualitative changes in skill patterns associated with the use of electronic telephone exchanges. In the Netherlands, for example, it has been estimated that the ratio of skilled to unskilled labour will change from 2:1, to 1:2. The demand for unskilled workers will increase by a factor of about four times.

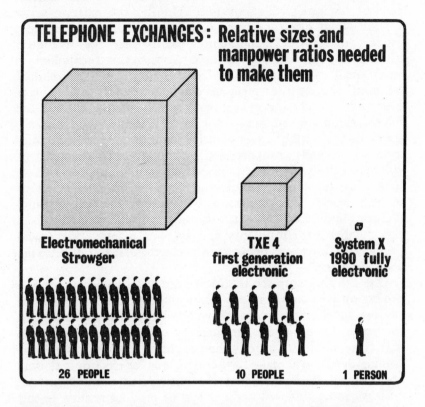

TELEPHONE EXCHANGES: Relative sizes and manpower ratios needed to make them

Electromechanical Strowger — 26 PEOPLE

TXE 4 first generation electronic — 10 PEOPLE

System X 1990 fully electronic — 1 PERSON

6(v) THE TEXTILE AND TEXTILE-MACHINERY INDUSTRIES

McLean and Rush (1978) have attempted to estimate the future possibilities and impact of the incorporation of microelectronics, and in particular microprocessors, in textile machinery in the U.K. They believe that there exists a good case for their rapid diffusion. First, electronic control systems clearly fulfil a useful function; they remove the need for labour and from the textile process, and labour costs still account for approximately one-third of total costs. Secondly, the historic pattern of

153

competition in the industry has been based on technical change and consequently the industry has displayed a high historic rate of technological innovation. Thirdly, the existing widespread use of electronics and conventional computing in most aspects of textile manufacture means that the 'technical distance' of the industry from microprocessor technology is very small. Fourthly, links have already been established between the textile machinery manufacturers and microelectronic and computer manufacturers. In particular DEC, the microcomputer manufacturers, have at present a virtual monopoly on the supply of computing equipment for both mill-monitoring and computerized knitting; with channels of communication already established we would suppose that at least this computer manufacturer would be attempting to actively market its products in the future to the textile manufacturing industry. There has also been considerable growth in the number of consultants and systems manufacturers who provide an interface between the electronics and the textile machine makers.

One can therefore see the future use of microelectronics as a projection of what has been happening up to now; in general the use of electronic controls will progress hand-in-hand with further increases in the productivity of textile machinery. In particular, the likely introduction of the multiphase loom in the coming decade will make further demands for electronic sensors and control devices so that the anticipated productivity increases can be achieved without loss of product quality. In this context a further development seems likely: at present electronic equipment incorporated into weaving machinery is essentially passive, and loom monitoring is performed by central computing equipment; modern microprocessor technology could enable fault detection and analysis to be performed locally by each production unit, making the process of mill-monitoring more effective. In the area of double jaquard knitting, where computer control of both machine operation and patterning has made the most progress, one would expect to see in the near future little further development due to the

154

peculiar market conditions. Such knitting machines at present are designed to work with synthetic fibres and the market for such machinery has been hit hard by the fashion swing towards fabrics made from natural fibres. There is consequently a tremendous surplus of secondhand electronically-controlled knitting machinery and little incentive for further technological improvement.

A further area in which the introduction of microprocessor control does seem likely is in the ink jet printing of tufted carpets. Tufted carpets now represent something like 60% of the market and there is tremendous incentive for the introduction of colour patterning. If such a process could be made commercially viable, and four systems using a crude version of this process have already been installed, then fashion would become incorporated in the market for carpets. Such a development could have serious consequences for the patterns of employment in the carpet-making industry. Tufted carpet production at present is already extremely capital intensive, the production process is relatively inflexible and produces large quantities of a very standardized product; the labour costs are thus largely incurred in stock holding and distribution. The introduction of tufted carpet patterning would inject a little labour back into the production process for monitoring and checking: on the other hand it would enable the carpet manufacturers to produce pattern carpets to particular customer orders and thus might result in a decrease in the labour requirement for stock holding and distribution.

There also seems to be enormous potential for the microprocessor control of processes which are in fact part of the garment industry (not strictly the textile industry), microprocessor-controlled laser cutting of patterns for garment manufacture shows indications of technical feasibility and would be both cheaper and more accurate than existing techniques. The increased accuracy of computer-controlled cutting techniques will also make possible a revolution in the processes involved in fitting these pieces together. Historic attempts to automate the garment-manufacturing process have failed due to the

155

extreme variability in the sizes of the pieces of material which have to be sewn together. Consequently a lot of skill is needed to make sure that the clothes come out the right size. Once the problem of the inaccurate size of pieces is overcome, then the computerized and automated production of garments should be quite feasible and extremely economic since garment manufacture is an extremely labour intensive process.

A lot more could be said about the potential detailed uses of microprocessors in the textile machinery industry. In summary, however, the pattern of future usage seems clear: that there will be few spectacular examples of automation using microelectronics in the textile industry itself but that the trend towards labour displacement will be continued and perhaps even accelerated. The potential for labour-saving innovations in the garment industry would seem to be tremendous.

Thus, in the textile industry proper, the changes in skill distribution already brought about through technical change, shown in Figure 6.3, are likely to intensify, with the proportion of highly-skilled and unskilled workers increasing at the expense of craft workers. At the same time, overall employment in the textile industry will continue to decline.

6(vi) MICROELECTRONICS AND AUTOMATION

Dickson and Marsh (1978) have, on the basis of a study by the American Society of Tool and Manufacturing Engineers, summarized the impacts of microelectronics associated with its applications to automated manufacture:
— A trend towards less skilled production line employment
— A reduction in certain job skills such as machining while an increase in other skills such as programmers and maintenance technicians
— Improved production consistency resulting in improved product quality at lower cost, thus giving rise to increase in customer satisfaction
— Manufacturers of production machinery benefit from

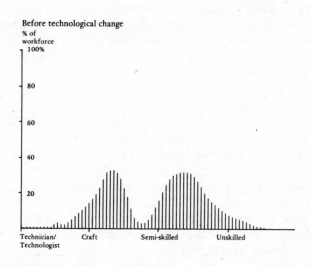

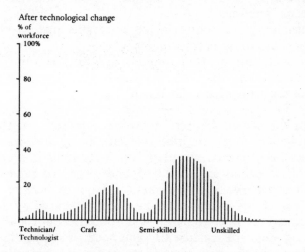

Source: The economic and employment aspects of technological change – John Fyfe (in Technology Choice and the future of work. BA symposium, November 22 1978).

Figure 6.3. Skill distribution in the textile industry.

reduced costs of standardized controls
- Improvements in flexible versatility due to reprogramm-ability of microelectronics controls will increase the design life of machine tools and will result in less reliance on expensive, purpose-built machinery
- Increasing emphasis on specialist support services, e.g. electronic maintenance staff
- Increase in labour productivity due to reduction in worker numbers, giving rise to structural unemployment
- A trend towards improved employment prospects for the more educated
- Structural unemployment will more likely affect, in the long term, the less educated employees
- Increase in trend towards more employment in service sector, especially those occupations not amenable to automation (e.g. catering, gardening)
- Generation of new management skills associated with 'systems' approach
- Restructuring of industrial organizations due to changing proportions of work roles and functions
- Reorganization of trade unions in order to suit new job structure.

According to Dickson and Marsh:

From this list of impacts it can be surmised that there are employment opportunities that are being lost as well as others being created; similarly there are skills that are being lost while others are generated, and so on. To achieve some balance between such alternatives requires perception and analysis of the extent of such effect generated by any new introduction of technology and some decision and policy-making apparatus sufficiently equipped to act on the results.

However, the importance attached to a particular effect, beneficial or otherwise, depends upon the nature of the interest of the observer. Government decisions, for example, are unlikely to prove popular with those sectors of society which do not directly benefit.

Dickson and Marsh then go on to describe the results of what they see as a major contribution to the forecasting and assessment of the impact of microelectronics on computer automation within manufacturing, carried out by the International Institution for Production Engineering Research (CIRP). Three key events related to the development of the computer-integrated factory are:

Event 1: By 1980 (median) a computer software system for full automation and optimization of all steps in the manufacturing of a part will be developed and in wide use.

Event 2: By 1985 (median), full on-line automation and optimization of complete manufacturing plants, controlled by a central computer, will be a reality.

Event 3: By 1990 (median), more than 50 per cent of the machine tools produced will not have a 'stand-alone' use, but will be part of a versatile manufacturing system, featuring automatic part handling between stations, and being controlled from a central process computer.

Using the Delphi methodology for obtaining a consensus scenario, members of CIRP were invited to assess the impact of the three events in terms of their economic, social and environmental consequences. In particular the participants were asked to give their opinion as to whether the occurrence of each of the events would have a beneficial effect, harmful effect or no effect on:

(i) the *economic* well-being of, in turn, factory workers, production engineers, universities, factories, countries

(ii) the *social* well-being of, in turn, factory workers, production engineers, universities, countries

(iii) the *environment* in, in turn, factories (noise, air, comfort, etc.), cities (air, traffic, crowding, etc.), the country-side (air, water, nature, etc.).

The results of this survey are presented in Table 6.1. From these it was concluded that there was a very strong consensus

Table 6.1. *Opinion Totals in CIRP Delphi-type Investigation of the Occurrence of Three Forecast Events Leading to the Realization of the Computer-integrated Automatic Factory*

| Effect | Opinion Totals | | | | | | | | |
| | Beneficial | | | Harmful | | | No effect | | |
Event No.	*1*	*2*	*3*	*1*	*2*	*3*	*1*	*2*	*3*
Economic effect on:									
factory workers	48	50	53	5	12	8	13	3	4
production engineers	61	61	61	0	1	1	4	3	3
universities	37	36	36	0	0	0	28	29	28
factories	57	57	60	4	5	2	1	0	0
countries	59	59	60	0	1	0	3	2	2
Social effect on:									
factory workers	40	37	40	15	24	19	10	3	5
production engineers	57	53	55	0	2	1	7	8	7
universities	6	7	6	0	0	0	57	56	57
countries	52	53	54	3	4	3	8	6	6
Environmental effect on:									
factories	50	52	56	3	4	3	10	7	4
cities	6	8	27	1	1	2	57	55	35
countryside	3	3	2	4	6	6	58	56	57

Key to Event Numbers:

Event 1   By 1980 (median), a computer software system for full automation and optimization of all steps in the manufacturing of a part will be developed and in wide use.

Event 2   By 1985 (median), full on-line automation and optimization of complete manufacturing plants, controlled by a central computer, will be a reality.

Event 3   By 1990 (median), more than 50% of the machine tools produced will not have a 'stand-alone' use, but will be part of a versatile manufacturing system, featuring automatic part handling between stations, and being controlled from a central process computer.

Source: Merchant M.E.; Technology Assessment of the Computer-integrated Automatic Factory, Annals of CIRP, Vol. 24/2, 1975, pp. 573–4.

that none of the three events would have a harmful economic effect on factory workers, production engineers, universities, factories or countries, and that they would have a beneficial economic effect on all these, with the possible exception of universities, and to a lesser degree, factory workers.

The consensus on the social impact was that none of the three events would have a harmful social effect on production engineers, universities or countries, and a reasonable consesnsus that they would have no harmful social effect on factory workers. There was a strong consensus that the social effect on production engineers and countries would be beneficial.

None of the three events was considered to have a harmful effect on the environment of factories, cities, or the country-side, and it was the majority view that they would have a beneficial effect on the environment of factories.

The report concluded that there was a very strong consensus that the coming of the computer-integrated automatic factory would in general have no harmful economic, social, or environmental effects, but that there was some significant doubt as to whether that was wholly true for the factory worker. A recommendation was made that the project be extended to explore the question of what action might be taken during the course of research leading to the three events in turn, with particular emphasis on Event 2, to ensure that no harmful economic or social effects on the factory worker occur.

6(vii) MICROELECTRONICS AND THE SELF-SERVICE ECONOMY

As pointed out in Chapter 3 of this book, during the post-war years there has been a marked growth in the 'self-service' economy. For example, television largely replaced cinema going as a form of visual entertainment, and the automatic washing machine has largely substituted for external laundry services.

161

With the event of cheap microprocessor controls, this trend is likely to intensify. Some examples of the potential impact of microelectronics device on services in the home are:
— the use of the television to provide a variety of information services;
— remote reading of gas and electricity meters;
— direct access to libraries;
— remote shopping and ordering;
— home electronic mail.

There are other areas in which microelectronics devices seem likely to intensify the trend towards self-service. One of the most important of these is medicine, and automatic blood pressure measuring machines already exist in the U.S.A. It might also establish a trend towards 'remote' diagnosis. Such a system already exists at Logan Field airport, Boston, where there is a well-equipped surgery and a nurse, but no on-the-spot doctor. The patient faces a set of TV cameras, describes his symptoms and has his blood pressure and other vital signs measured by the nurse: the doctor (based at Massachusetts General Hospital) can use a stethoscope to listen to the patient's chest and study an electrocardiagram sent over the wires direct to his office in the hospital. According to Martin (1978) medicine by remote control is exactly what many doctors want, and it could greatly improve medical services in remote country areas.

6(viii) SUMMARY

The case studies presented in this chapter have highlighted a number of important factors relating to the use of microprocessors in the manufacturing and service sectors:
— In those instances where electronic controls are already in use — e.g. textile machinery, automation in manufacturing — the effect of microelectronics will be primarily to *intensify existing trends*, i.e. further reduce already declining manning levels, further reduce traditional skill requirements. In these cases failure to adopt the new technology will result in

162

greater job loss in the longer term through lack of international technical change competitiveness.

— In several other areas, the impact of microelectronics is likely to be much greater. In the case of the newspaper industry, for example, the adoption of modern printing technology not only significantly reduces overall manpower requirements, but also renders certain traditional craft skills redundant. In the case of office work, once again the adoption of microelectronic technology will have a very great impact in that productivity will be doubled and the nature of office tasks changed. Here, however, the impact in the short term at least appears to be positive in that employment increases slightly, and the secretary's job is enriched. In the longer term, though, demand for office staff will fail to increase as in the past, and a pattern of jobless growth will be established.*

— In the case of the self-service economy, the impact of microelectronics will be to broaden the range of 'self-services' available, with subsequent job loss in the 'final services' sector.

— Microelectronics devices can provide opportunities for generating employment in progressive firms. This was shown in the case of the West German printing firm. *Overall* employment in the industry is — in the absence of accelerated growth in demand — likely, however, to fall.

— In the case of the watchmaking industry, while global employment declined as a result of the use of microcircuitry, job loss was relatively greatest in the traditional watch making countries which failed to adopt the new technology.

— In firms manufacturing microelectronics-based equipment (e.g. telecommunications industry) jobs will be lost on a substantial scale for an equivalent output (see the Appendix to this chapter).

— Finally, as more and more workers and managers see both the existence and the nature of their jobs threatened by the new

---

*This is already apparent in banking. In the May 1979 *National Westminster Bank Review*, Haslam has shown that, mainly due to the use of electronics technology, while the volume of business has increased since 1970 by 7% per annum, employment has increased by a total of only 7% during the same period.

163

technology, reaction against its adoption is likely to increase. Reaction will vary between industrial cultures and will cause the balance between the job-generating effect and the job-destruction effect of employment to differ from country to country.

APPENDIX*

The impact of microelectronics on assembly and negative multiplier effects

Impact of microelectronics on assembly

Microelectronic-based circuits can substitute for a large proportion of assembled devices commonly used throughout the economy, such as electromechanical meters, switchgear, complex assembled circuits such as subsystems of radios and TVs, and the other measurement, monitoring and control devices currently utilizing any mix of mechanical, electromechanical, electric, discrete or integrated circuit technology. It is a characteristic of the production technology of such current devices that the labour density pattern of activities involved in production is roughly pyramidal in shape, with relatively large numbers of low skills at the base activities, and smaller numbers of higher skills† near the top of the pyramid. A typical distribution could be:

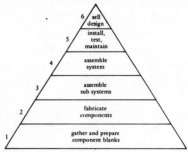

*Taken from Barron and Curnow, 1979.

†By contrasting high/low skills we imply only skills requiring more/less training, or adaptive/rote based.

This activity density pattern is product based, not necessarily firm based. Thus in car manufacturers British Leyland is chiefly a 4, 5, 6 company, but with agents carrying out much of 5; levels 1, 2, 3 in this case are networks of suppliers who often supply other car assemblers also. At a more elemental level, screws, rivets, paxolin boards, wires, discrete components, are bought in for electrical circuit assembly by a 4, 5, 6 electrical product manufacturer.

In order to control this pyramid of activity, managerial and technical skills are also required. A characteristic of both is that with this type of activity the span of managerial or technical skill need not extend through the whole multilayered pyramid; it is currently sufficient if such skills merely bridge adjacent layers:

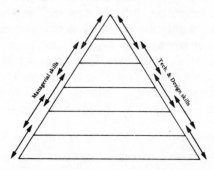

However, the nature of both the design process and production process of a microelectronic circuit is such that this structure is totally altered. For example, the next figure shows the part of the pyramid totally displaced by an LSI circuit, and the corresponding requirement for span of managerial and

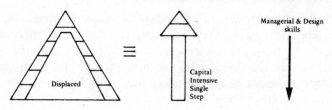

design skill. It also indicates diagrammatically the nature of the labour displacement effected, when such substitution is possible. From this conceptual diagram, plus the earlier point that such devices are cheaper, more reliable than the devices they displace, plus the additional point that they are individually less material and energy intensive, we can start to structure the likely employment effects.

Negative multiplier inside electronic firms

The semiconductor suppliers themselves, will, for equivalent output, become less labour intensive, and at full production with a stable production technology, less capital intensive.

Those firms with activities, 1–2–3 and part 4, will have such activities displaced by the availability of LSI circuits embodying such activities, whether such circuits are bought in or manufactured. These essentially assembly activities will be displaced by an activity involving less capital, vastly decreased labour input, less supervision, less space, less administration.

The maintenance and repair of such devices again will require substantially reduced labour, reduced capital content for diagnostic equipment, and again reduced economic activity.

Negative multiplier for suppliers to electronic firms

Since the products and process equipment incorporation microelectronic elements are more powerful in their performance, it follows that for the same performance or output requirement, less product or equipment is required, and there must be a corresponding drop in the labour required to replenish the stock of products or equipment in use.

Negative impact upstream to such suppliers

Since the substituting circuits are less material intensive, and less energy intensive, they are also less handling, machining, forming and fabrication intensive, and there is a corresponding reduction in the need for equipment to perform those functions, with the concomitant reduction in labour required to produce such equipment.

166

CHAPTER 7

SUMMARY OF MAIN POINTS

The phenomenon of jobless growth has become well established in the agricultural sectors of the advanced economies during the past few decades mainly as a result of technical change. Until fairly recently displaced agricultural workers have been absorbed in industrial production and in services.

Since the mid-1960s, and more notably so since 1973, there has been decreasing employment in industrial production in most of the advanced economies. Despite growth in industrial output, which has occurred following the 1974–75 recession, employment in production has continued to decrease. The phenomenon of jobless growth has now also become established in the goods-producing sectors of the advanced economies caused mainly through technological change. Indeed since the beginning of the 1970s, new industrial investment — in Europe at least — has moved away from new product development and expansion and moved increasingly towards rationalization investment. High wages and high rates of social benefits have been major factors in stimulating this shift.

Companies have also been — and are being — forced into this rationalization process by international price competitiveness factors. This response has involved the scaling-up of operations and the adoption of capital-intensive labour-saving technology. Firms have also 'exported' employment by relocating their plants into regions of low labour costs.

In some areas demand factors have also been important in

167

creating unemployment. In the steel industry, for example, many jobs have been lost due to the fall in world demand for steel during and after the 1974–75 recession. In shipbuilding numerous jobs are being lost due to lack of demand for ships. In a number of consumer goods there is market saturation.

In the less competitive of the advanced economies, many jobs have been lost – at least in the capital goods industries in Europe – through lack of technical change competitiveness in the face of technically superior products produced in other advanced countries. In the case of the EEC the rate of displacement has also been affected by rationalization within EEC countries.

Thus, competition in some areas is based mainly on making standard products cheaper. In this case the major thrust of technical change is of the process rationalization kind. In other areas, e.g. capital goods, non-price factors are dominant in competitiveness; here 'technical change' (product quality and performance) competition dominates.

The above factors (technical change rationalization, demand, low wage cost competition) by no means act exclusively within specific sectors or economies. In the steel industry, for example, jobs have been lost through a fall in demand, technical change rationalization and, in some countries, lack of international technical change competitiveness. In textiles (mainly clothing) jobs have been lost as the result of both competition from low wage cost areas, and through labour-saving technical change.

The most important single recent technical change which has affected employment throughout manufacturing has been the application of electronics.

The use of electronic controls in manufacturing has resulted in both *loss* of employment and *changes* in skill distribution. New, high-level electronics and software skills have been required, while some craft skills have been made largely redundant. Overall there has been a great deal of craft de-skilling, with an increased requirement for on-the-job training. It has also imposed the need for management to acquire higher level technical skills.

168

The application of microelectronics will intensify both these trends in the manufacturing sector. However, failure to adopt microelectronics technologies will lead to a reduction in international competitiveness on the part of the individual firms or countries concerned.

Also over the past decades employment in both the public and private service sectors has increased very substantially. Although the private service sector has a substantial potential for growth, the slight productivity increases experienced in the past, its present generally low capital intensity, and the potential of mainly microelectronics to greatly increase productivity, make it likely that labour absorption in this sector will be coming to an end. An additional jobless growth sector will evolve.

The use of microelectronics is also likely to intensify the trend towards the self-service economy. This will add to loss in employment in the final services sector.

Companies manufacturing microcircuits, and those using microelectronics in their equipment will, for the same output potential, require less labour (negative multiplier effect). The same will be true for suppliers of components and sub-assemblies. Thus, for equivalent output, the use of microelectronics will result in a reduction in global employment in a given sector (e.g. watch manufacturing). However, as well as destroying or degrading employment, the use of microelectronics can offer *opportunities* for firms to produce new, innovative products.

Previous experience with the use of electronics (i.e. computers) in the service sector has shown that the widespread adoption of new technology takes place over a period of many years and has resulted, in the first instance, in an increase in employment. The negative employment impact of microprocessors is not, therefore, likely to manifest itself in the short term. However, its somewhat longer-term consequences for service employment are immense.

There generally exists a growing mis-match between skills and job opportunities. The adoption of microelectronics devices

169

is likely to increase this mis-match in the absence of comprehensive retraining schemes. Because of this, and because of their employment destroying effect, growing objections from both workers and management might significantly slow down the rate of adoption of new technologies. This resistance is liable to vary from country to country. Industries and countries which opt for short-term job protection by resisting new technology will, in the longer term, suffer greater job loss through lack of international technical change competitiveness. Lack of technical expertise on the part of management might also significantly retard the adoption of the new technology, as occurred with NC machine tools in the U.K.

Further, with Californian referendum-style thinking increasing on both sides of the Atlantic, coupled to pressures for wages parity in the public service sector, it seems unlikely that governments will be free to expand public services in order to soak up significant numbers of the unemployed.

To take advantage of new technology in order to creat jobs, governments in the advanced economies should develop policies to stimulate companies to embark on more vigorous programmes to develop new products in both existing and in new firms. In the light of a recent study by Birch (1979), which showed that two-thirds of all new jobs in industry in the U.S. came from companies employing fewer than twenty people, and that no fewer than four-fifths of all new jobs come from firms less than 5 years old (and supported by the recent study by the U.S. Department of Commerce*), governments should pay increased attention to offering incentives towards, and creating the right environment for, the creation of many new small firms.

A number of the government policies that can affect both the rate and the direction of technical change, both of which have an impact on the relationship between technical change and employment, have been described in some detail in previous reports prepared within the Six Countries Programme.

This, and other work, is aimed at providing insight into prob-

*See footnote, page 57.

lems of technical change and at evaluating and describing policies that would both foster and direct technical change.

It should be noted that important changes in factor costs including labour, raw materials, energy and capital will have a substantial impact on both the direction and the rate of technical change and hence on employment.

It is with this consideration in mind that the conclusions of this report as to the future should be interpreted.

References

Aubert, J. A. (1978), 'Innovation and Unemployment: Towards A Cultural Reading', Six Countries Workshop, Paris, November 13-14.

Barnett, C. J. *et al.* (1978), *Industrial Automation − Its Nature, Effects and Management*, Critical Issues Report, CPA 78-17, CPA, MIT, September.

Barron, T. and Curnow, R. (1979), *The Future with Microelectronics*, Frances Pinter (Publishers) Ltd, London.

Beckmann, G. and Vahrenkamp, R. (1978), 'The Industrialisation of the Service Sector: the Case of Computer Aided Design (CAD)', Six Countries Workshop, Paris, November 13-14.

Birch, D. L. (1979), *The Job Generation Process*, Research Report, MIT, Center for Policy Alternatives.

Blaxter, K. L. (1973), 'The Limites to Agricultural Improvement', Lecture, University of Newcastle Agricultural Society, December 10.

Branscomb, L. M. (1979), 'The Electronics Revolution: Micro Circuits and Macro Challenges', Paper presented at the United States Embassy, London, January 15.

Central Policy Review Staff (1978), *Social Implications of Micro-electronics*, London, November.

Clark, J. A. (1978), 'Economic Interpretations of the Relation between Technical Change and Unemployment', Staff/Unitar Working Paper, November (Science Policy Research Unit).

Cohen-Hadria, Y. (1978), 'Automation and Work-Integration in Cement Industries', Six Countries Workshop, Paris, November 13-14.

Coriat, B. (1978), 'Différenciation et Segmentation de la Force de Travail dans les Industries de Procès', in La Division du Travail, *Actes Colloque de Dourdau*, Ed. Galitée, Paris.

Cox, J. C. (1978), 'Technical Development and Employment − Problems of Keynesian Economics', Six Countries Workshop, Paris, November 13-14.

Dickson, K. and March, J. (1978), *The Micro-electronics Revolution; a Brief Assessment of the Industrial Impact with a Selected Bibliography*, Occasional Paper, Technology Policy Unit, University of Aston in Birmingham.

Financial Times (1979), 'The Printing Industry', Tuesday, January 23 (Roy Coxhead).

*Papers presented at the Six Countries Programme Workshop in Paris, November 1978, can be obtained from W. Zegveld, Staffgroup Strategic Surveys, TNO, P.O. Box 215, Delft, Netherlands.

Financial Times (1979), 'Unions Keep a Watchful Eye on New Technology', Tuesday, January 23 (P. Jaspert).

Freeman, C. (1977), 'The Kondratiev Long Waves, Technical Change and Unemployment', OECD Conference, Structural Determinants of Employment and Unemployment, March 7-11, Paris.

Freeman, C. (1978), 'Technical Change and Future Employment Prospects in Industrialized Societies', Six Countries Workshop, Paris, November 13-14.

Freeman, C. and Curnow, R. (1978), 'Technical Change and Employment – A Review of Post-War Research'. Paper prepared for Manpower Services Commission (Science Policy Research Unit), June.

Fuchs, W. R. (1978), *The Service Economy*, National Bureau of Economic Research Inc., New York.

Gershuny, J. I. (1979), 'The Informal Economy: its Role in the post-industrial Society', *Futures*, February.

Glismann, H. H., Rodemer, H., and Water, F. (1978), 'Zur Natur der Wachstumschawache in der BRD, eine empirishe Analyse langer Zyklen wirtschaftlicher Entwicklung', Kieler Institut für Weltwirtschaft, June.

Goodacre, C. (1979) 'Roland's Computer Controlled Inking', *Printing Equipment and Materials*, Vol. 17, No. 179.

Harman, W. W. (1978), 'Chronic Unemployment: An Emerging Problem of Post-Industrial Society', *The Futurist*, August.

Haslam, J. (1979), 'An Appraisal of Microelectronic Technology', *Nat. West. Bank Quarterly Review*, May.

Hepworth, R., Kelly, A., Stokoe, A., Wellians, S., Weaver, J., Welsh, M., and McCornick, K. (1967), 'Effects of Technical Change in the Yorkshire Coalfield between 1957 and 1965' in *Studies in the British Coal Industry* (Eds.), D. Kelley and D. Forsyth, Economic Studies Publication Group, London.

Jacobson, L. (1978), 'Employment Effects of Technological Change in the Steel Industry', Six Countries Programme Workshop, Paris, November 13-14.

Kanters, B. (1978), 'Technical Change in Industry and Qualitative Labour Market Problems', Six Countries Workshop, Paris, November 13-14.

Kuznets, S. (1940), 'Review of Business Cycles', *American Economic Review*, Volume 30, June.

Little, A. D., Ltd (1977) *New Technology-based Firms in the United Kingdom and the Federal Republic of Germany*, Wilton House Publications Ltd.

Maddock, I., C.B., O.B.E., F.R.S. (1978), 'The Future of Work', *Technology Choice and the Future of Work*, One day Symposium, Wednesday, 22 November. British Association for the Advancement of Science, London.

Mensch, G. (1978), '1984: A New Push of Basic Innovations?', *Research Policy*, 7.

Lund, R. T. *et al.* (1978), *Numerically Controlled Machine Tools and Group Technology: A study of U.S. Experiences*, Report CPA, 78-2, January 13, CPA, MIT.

Martin, J. (1978), *The Wired Society*, Prentice Hall.

McLean, J. M. and Rush, H. J. (1978), *The Impact of Micro-electronics on the U.K.: A suggested Classification and Illustrative Case Study*, SPRU Occasional Paper Series, No. 7.

Meadows, E. (1978), 'Productivity Lag', *Fortune*, December 4.

N.S.F. (1978), 'To-day's View Clips', September 29 (Public Information Branch, OGPP).

Parkinson, B. (1978), 'The Buyer's Approach to Word Processor Systems', Seminar,

The London International Press Centre, April 19 and 20.

Peitchinis, S. G. (1978), 'Technology and Employment in Industry and Services', Six Countries Workshop, Paris, November 13-14.

Ray, G. F. (1979), 'Some Economic Aspects of Innovation', Paper presented to: Conference on Innovation Studies in the U.K., Anglian Regional Management Centre, Danbury, May 31 and June 1.

Remmerswaal, J. (1978), 'Production Technology in the Metal Working Industry and Employment', Six Countries Workshop, Paris, November 13-14.

Rothwell, R. (1976), *Innovation in Textile Machinery: Some Significant Factors in Success and Failure*, SPRU, Occasional Paper Series, No. 2, June.

Rothwell, R. (1977), 'The Role of Technical Change in International Competitiveness: The Case of the Textile Machinery Industry', *Management Decision*, Vol. 15, No. 3.

Rothwell, R. (1978), 'Where Britain Lags Behind', *Management To-day*, November.

Schumpeter, J. (1939), *Business Cycles*, New York.

Soete, L. (1978), 'International Competition, Innovation and Employment', Six Countries Workshop, Paris, November 13-14.

Stark, J. (1978), 'Hold the Front Frame', *New Scientist*, November 30.

Swards-Isherwood, N. and Senker, P. (1978a), 'Automated Small Batch Production', NEL, DoI, London (Science Policy Research Unit).

Swards-Isherwood, N. and Senker, P. (1978b), 'Automation in the Engineering Industry', *Labour Research*, November.

Townsend, J. F. (1976), *Innovation in Coal Mining Machinery: The Anderton Shearer Loader — the Role of the NCB and the Supply Industry in its Development*, SPRU Occasional Paper Series No. 3, December.

Vandoorne, M. and Meeusen, W. (1978), *The Clay-Clay Vintage Model as an Approach to the Structural Unemployment in Belgian Manufacturing: A first Exploration of the Theoretical and Structural Problems*, Antwerp University, State University Centre, Antwerp, Working Paper 78-08.

Van Rossem, J. P. (1978), *Hoe ziek is onze Ekonomie? Anatomie van de ekonomische krises in België*, VPRO.

Wilkinson, M. (1978), 'System X: The Need to Shake-up the "phone-makers" ', *Financial Times*, Wednesday, October 18.

INDEX

absenteeism, 122
adaptive control, 109
aerodynamics, 79
aggregate demand, 3, 4, 9, 48, 107, 128, 131
aggregate demand theory, 15, 16, 56
agriculture, 3, 12, 37, 39, 41, 62
Aleixo, Al, 148, 149
American Society of Tool and Manu-
    facturing Engineers, 156
American trade unions, 2
Anderton Shearer-Leader (ASL), 68
Anglo-German Foundation, 56
Aubert, J. A., 58
automated office, 142, 143
automation, 2, 29, 61, 98, 99, 100, 101, 103, 112, 113, 114, 117, 120, 122, 123, 124, 125, 126, 127, 128, 129, 138, 142, 143, 144, 156, 159

Barron, I., 142, 147
basic oxygen furnace, 105
Beckmann, G., 118, 119, 120, 121
Belgium, 53
Bernett, C. J., 122
Bethlehem Steel, 57
Branscomb, L. M., 145
Brazil, 5
British Leyland, 145, 165
British management, 116
British Steel Corporation (BSC), 106, 107

Brozen, Yale, 126
Bulgaria, 5

calculators, 29
Californian referendum, 9, 48
Canadian Railways, 76, 79, 131, 132
capital goods industries, 7, 26
capital intensive electronic processes, 45
capital investment, 45
'capital shortage' unemployment, 9, 10, 12
carpet-making industry, 155
Carrington Viyella, 92, 94
cement, 97, 98, 101, 102, 103
Central Policy Review Staff, 138, 145
Centre for Policy Alternatives, 124
chemicals, 5, 6, 24
chemical technology, 79
chip, 33
civil service, 138, 139, 144, 146
Clark, J. A., 15
clothing, 24
coal, 68
coal industry, 68, 72, 74
coal mining, 131
coal mining industry, 67, 70, 76
Cohen-Hadria, Y., 97, 98, 101
Combined English Mills (CEM), 92, 94
communications technology, 11
computer, 29, 32, 97, 109, 113, 114, 116, 120, 121, 128, 138, 139, 144, 146, 149, 150, 152, 159

computer-aided design, 113, 118, 119, 120, 121, 122
computer bureaux, 32
computer-controlled cutting techniques, 155
computer-controlled drills, 135
computer-controlled production systems, 112
computer-integrated automatic factory, 161
computerization, 61
Coriat, B., 102
cost-saving rationalization, 10
Cox, J. C., 41
Curnow, R., 137, 142, 147
'cyclical' unemployment, 15
Czechoslovakia, 80

data processing, 98, 144
Delphi methodology, 159
demographic changes, 8
'developing countries', 5
Dickson, K., 156, 158, 159
digital equipment, 57

education, 8, 44, 45, 55, 116
electronically-controlled knitting machinery, 155
electronic data processing (EDP), 45, 119, 120
electronic equipment, 11
electronic revolution, 137
electronics, 29, 34, 76, 79, 95, 140, 154
electronic sensors, 154
electronic technology, 46, 47, 48
employment, 2, 3, 4, 7, 8, 9, 11, 16, 17, 37, 38, 41, 53, 60, 74, 77, 79, 80, 83, 92, 95, 104, 108, 110, 117, 122, 129, 133, 138, 139, 158, 164, 168
energy, 68, 131, 166
England, 64
entrepreneurs, 10
Europe, 1, 2, 3, 4, 5, 7, 8, 32, 48, 57, 58, 66, 107, 118, 167, 168
European Economic Community, 18, 20, 66, 107, 168

Financial Times, 146, 147

First World War, 28
food, 4, 24
Ford, 66
France, 37, 53, 106, 126, 131
Freeman, C., 17, 28, 29, 34, 47, 137
Fuchs, W. R., 41, 44, 46

gas, 68
General Motors, 57
German economy, 27
Gershuny, J. I., 43, 49
Glass Houghton Colliery, 73, 74
Glismann, H. H., 27
Goodacre, C., 151
Great Britain, 126
Greece, 5
group technology, 113
group-technology systems, 112

Harman, W. W., 58
Hepworth, R., 71
high wage economies, 6
human capital, 12

Iceland, 25
immigrant labour, 96
India, 5
industrial revolution, 123
'information based' power, 125
information-flow, 113, 114, 143
information technology, 57, 145
ink jet printing, 155
International Business Machines (IBM), 57, 138, 145
International Institution for Production Engineering Research (CIRP), 159
international price competition, 7
Italy, 53

Japan, 3, 4, 24, 32, 37, 53, 57, 138
job dissatisfaction, 122, 123
jobless growth, 8, 38, 41, 126, 146, 163, 167, 169
Journal Bulletin, 148, 150

Kanters, B., 59
Keynesian demand stimulation methods, 18
'knowledge-based' power, 125

Kondratiev, 26, 27, 28, 29
Kondratiev cycles, 27, 29
Kondratiev-type cycle, 34
Kondratiev's waves, 28
Korea, 5
Kovoslav National Corporation, 80
Kuznets, S., 27

labour-intensive industries, 20
labour-intensive processes, 45, 84
labour-intensive techniques, 6
labour-saving change, 17
labour-saving plant, 41
labour-saving technical change, 7, 10
large scale integrated circuits (LSIs), 33
less developed countries, 96
long-wave theory, 26
Little (A. D.) Ltd., 56
low wage cost countries (LDCs), 20, 21, 25
Lund, R. T., 114

machinery, 24
Maddock, I., 133
Marion Labs, 57
Marsh, J., 156, 158, 159
Martin, J., 162
mature industrialized societies, 1
mature technological societies, 7, 12
McCracken Report, 10
McLean, J. M., 140, 153
mechanical engineering, 6
Meeusen, W., 18
Mensch, G., 27
metals, 5, 24
Mexico, 5
microelectronics, 56, 57, 109, 132, 133, 136, 137, 138, 139, 141, 145, 152, 153, 154, 156, 158, 159, 161, 162, 164, 169
microcircuitry, 163
microcomputers, 11
microcomputer manufacturers, 154
microelectronically-controlled plant, 133
microelectronic revolution, 10
microelectronics-based control systems, 146
microprocessor, 33, 117, 122, 146, 153, 154, 155, 156, 162
microprocessor-based office systems, 139
microprocessor-controlled inking systems, 151
microprocessor-controlled laser cutting, 155
mineral, 24
mining, 3, 12

National Cash Register, 33
neoclassical economists, 16
neo-Marxist, 16, 17
Netherlands, 4, 53, 58, 59, 152
newspaper industry, 163
New York Times, 126
New Zealand, 25
North America, 5
numerically controlled (NC) machine tools, 114, 115, 116, 117, 118, 131

OECD, 2, 10, 18, 25, 37, 38, 39, 43, 53, 55, 56, 126, 127
OPEC, 4

Peitchinis, S. G., 44, 46, 48, 76, 77, 79
petro-chemical industry, 102
petroleum products, 24
photosetting, 146
Polaroid, 57
polyvalency, 100, 101, 102, 103, 129
'post-industrial' society, 4
printing, 6, 11
printing industry, 146, 147, 151
private sector service activities, 11
Providence Typographical Union, 148
public sector employment, 47
publishing, 11

Ray, G. F., 28
Reiff & Co., 151
Remmerswaal, J., 109, 110, 113
REPCO Selftwist System, 92
robotized assembly systems, 113
Rodemar, H., 27
Rothwell, R., 79, 80, 81
rubber, 6, 24
Rush, H. J., 140, 153

Schumpeter, J., 17, 26, 27, 28
Scotland, 64, 74
Second World War, 28, 29, 34, 66, 67, 80, 133
semiconductor industry, 57
semiconductor suppliers, 166
Senker, P., 116
Shepard, 125
shipbuilding, 6, 58
Soete, L., 17, 24
software, 131, 159
spinning, 86, 89, 90, 92
steel, 6, 68, 103, 105, 106, 107
Stork, J., 148
structural change, 4, 12, 38
structural change theory, 16, 20
structural employment, 25, 158
'structuralist', 2, 9
structural unemployment, 12, 15, 16, 26, 55, 128
Sulzer Brothers, 80
Sulzer Flying Gripper Weaving Machine, 80
Sweden, 53, 54, 55
Switzerland, 138
Swords-Isherwood, N., 116
synthetic fibres, 155

Taiwan, 5
technical change, 5, 6, 11, 12, 15, 24, 25, 26, 28, 29, 32, 50, 68, 76, 79, 80, 83, 84, 92, 103, 105, 107, 129, 131, 140, 142, 154, 156, 163, 167, 168
technical change competitiveness, 106
technological change, 46, 71, 73, 74, 86, 89, 90, 113, 167
technological unemployment, 72, 133
technology, 2, 11, 29, 45, 60, 61, 95, 105, 108, 114, 118, 122, 123, 124, 126, 131, 132, 133, 134, 136, 137, 138, 140, 141, 147, 151, 154, 158, 163, 164, 166, 167, 170

telecommunications industry, 152, 163
teletype, 120
textile, 4, 5, 24, 58, 80, 81, 95, 153, 154, 156, 168
textile industry, 83, 84, 96
textile machinery industry, 79, 153, 156
textile manufacturing industry, 154
transport, 24

United Kingdom, 4, 34, 39, 53, 55, 56, 62, 63, 66, 67, 68, 70, 80, 83, 84, 94, 106, 107, 116, 118, 131, 138, 140, 142, 147, 152, 153, 170
United States, 1, 2, 3, 4, 5, 8, 9, 18, 24, 25, 32, 41, 47, 48, 53, 55, 56, 57, 58, 61, 64, 103, 107, 114, 118, 126, 129, 139, 140, 162, 170
U.S. Domestic Policy Review on Innovation, 1
U.S. National Commission on Technology, Automation and Economic Progress, 2

Vahrenkamp, R., 118, 119, 120, 121
Vandoorne, M., 18
Van Rossem, J. P., 16
Vietnam War, 61

'wave-theory' of innovation, 26
Western Electric, 34
Western Europe, 34, 54, 55, 80, 81, 96
Western World, 110, 113
West Germany, 53, 55, 56, 106, 116, 120, 126, 131
Wilkinson, M., 152
Wolter, F., 27
wood, 24
word processing, 138, 140, 141, 142, 146
word processors, 11, 142, 145, 146

Xerox Corporation, 141

Yugoslavia, 5